GW00746204

The
Bare Necessities
of
Faith

Other books by David M. Adams.

The Bare Necessities of Faith.

Seek My Face - the biblical basis of seeking the Lord

The
Bare Necessities
of
Faith

DAVID M. ADAMS

RPP
ROPERPENBERTHY PUBLISHING

Published by RoperPenberthy Publishing Ltd
PO Box 545, Horsham, RH12 4QW

First Published 2001

ISBN 1 903905 06-0

Printed in the United Kingdom.

PREFACE

There is a huge literature on 'faith', so why write another book about it? I have read many books on faith, and sat under some wonderful and inspiring teaching on it by 'big names'. Yet when I came to teach it myself I discovered that my own grasp and understanding of it was far more tenuous and patchy than I had realised.

I went back to several books on faith that had helped me but the deeper I pressed certain questions, the more confused I became. In the end I abandoned them all and did what I have always done in my work as a research scientist: I went back to the basic data and let them tell their own story. I downloaded from my Bible software every reference to faith. I then arranged them by topic, meditated on them, prayed for God's wisdom (James 1:5-6), and began to write. Revelation flowed under the Spirit's inspiration! Then I added quotations from my reading on faith that have helped me personally. I hope you will enjoy them too.

Everyone who teaches knows that what you actually present on a given subject hangs upon a basic logical framework that exists in your mind at all times and is continually refined in the light of new revelation. This book represents an attempt to present in summary what has become my framework of the meaning of biblical faith. I have tried to highlight the operative principles and thereby to provide a logical foundation which can be elaborated by each reader from his own study and experience. So as to allow the logical structure to stand out, I have avoided the temptation to lard this structure with stories: you can do that for yourself.

My debt to many authors and teachers is immense and obvious, but I owe an especial debt of gratitude to Dr John McKay (Kingdom Faith Ministries) for sharpening my understanding of some key issues. Naturally, I alone bear responsibility for all views expressed and for any remaining errors.

In some cases I have been unable to trace the precise source of what I have quoted: I ask forgiveness and understanding where that is the case. I am most grateful to David Higham for making up the Figures for Chapter 6. Some questions and suggestions for further study are given. In view of the widespread availability of Bible-study software, I have also included some computer-based exercises.

David M. Adams

Leicester, UK
January 2001

CONTENTS

CHAPTER 1.

The Basic Features of Faith

Preview: In this Chapter biblical faith is first contrasted with natural faith. In scripture the word 'faith' is used in three contexts: to refer to (1) entry into God's kingdom; (2) the normal Christian lifestyle; and (3) that body of doctrine, 'The Faith', which defines Christian belief. The distinction between faith and believing is made.

Introduction.

Faith is at the heart of Christianity. We enter God's kingdom by faith in his Son, Jesus Christ, and we are to live out our lives as his disciples - by faith.

By grace you have been saved through faith. (Ephesians 2:8)

For in the gospel a righteousness from God is revealed,
a righteousness that is by faith from first to last,
just as it is written: "The righteous will live by faith."
(Romans 1:17)

Just as you received Christ Jesus as Lord,
continue to live in him. (Colossians 2:6)

In the scriptures we find that the sick are healed and the demonised set free; the dead raised, prison doors opened and weather modified - all by faith. Indeed, it turns out that: everything that does not come from faith is sin (*Romans 14:23*), and that without faith it is impossible to please God (*Hebrews 11:6*), yet to many Christians faith remains an elusive and puzzling thing.

"To many Christians, faith is their own ability to believe
a promise or a truth, and is often based upon their
struggles to drive away doubt and unbelief through
a process of continuous affirmations." (Charles Price)

Stories of great faith exploits written by men and women of God excite and inspire us, but at the same time can lead us to conclude that the gap between their great faith and our little faith is too large to be bridged. We really do want to please God but - how are we to operate with that kind of faith?

Natural faith and biblical faith.

Since scripture declares that everything in the Christian's life is to be by faith, it follows that faith must be simple to understand, not complicated or difficult of access. Let us encourage ourselves at the outset by appreciating that all our lives are already lived by faith, whether or not we are Christians. It is an act of faith to believe that the chair I am about to sit on will support me; that this tin of baked beans contains what the label says; and that the train timetable is sufficiently reliable that I can plan my movements around it. Life cannot be lived without the continual exercise of 'natural faith'. The exercise of faith is as natural as breathing.

The Bible shows that the natural is but a reflection of the supernatural. Hence, it should not surprise us that our life in God is also to be by faith, a supernaturally natural faith, and therefore that Jesus expected to find faith in those who came to him. He still does.

What is the difference between 'natural faith' and 'biblical faith'? 'Biblical faith' is in God himself, whereas 'natural faith' is in something else (the chair; the manufacturer of the tin of beans; the train company). So as we start this study, be encouraged that you're almost certainly much farther down the faith track than you give yourself credit for. Glory to God!

Faith is a relationship, not a mechanism.
Our aim in this study is to reveal the operative principles of biblical faith, and to present thereby a logical framework upon which you can hang your own experience and understanding. However, it must be said at the outset that faith is not a mechanism but a relationship, and in relationships heart issues are paramount. So then, as we study together, let us ask the Holy Spirit to bring a greater revelation of Jesus into our hearts, so that we also may learn to move in great faith, and fulfil the high calling of God upon our lives.

> *Faith is being sure of what we hope for and*
> *certain of what we do not see. (Hebrews 11:1)*

"Faith is the spiritual faculty of the soul which deals with the spiritual realities of the future and the unseen." (Andrew Murray)[1]

"Faith is God perceived by the heart." (Oswald Chambers)

"Faith is the biblical word for the human response to God's grace." (I. Howard Marshall)[2]

"The purpose of faith is to serve God, not ourselves. Every area that we use our faith should bring glory to God." (Andrew Wommack)[3]

Three aspects of faith.

The New Testament (NT) uses the concept of faith in three distinct but related contexts.

1. Justifying (or saving) faith. We enter God's kingdom by repentance and faith in Jesus Christ as Son of God. This first experience of biblical faith brings us into a living relationship with Jesus Christ. By this faith we are justified, made righteous, holy and acceptable in God's sight, and are able to enter his presence with confidence. Not only are our sins forgiven, we ourselves are forgiven! Moreover, we are saved from ourselves, from the corrupt 'old man', our sinful and selfish lifestyle, which has now been nailed to the cross with Christ. Both this double salvation from sin and self, and the faith by which it is made possible, are God's gift to us.

For it is by grace you have been saved, through faith
—and this not from yourselves, it is the gift of God
— not by works, so that no one can boast. (Ephesians 2:8-9)

Saving is all his idea, and all his work. All we do is
trust him enough to let him do it. It's God's gift from
start to finish! We don't play the major role. If we did,
we'd probably go about bragging that we'd done
the whole thing! (Ephesians 2:8-9, The Message)

We ... know that a man is not justified by observing
the law, but by faith in Jesus Christ. (Galatians 2:16)

If you are a Christian, if you have repented of your sins

and of your former way of life, have asked Jesus, the Son of God, to forgive you and to be Lord of your life from now on, then it follows that **you already have justifying faith.**

"The Invisible takes the initiative and wakens faith."
(Andrew Murray)[4]

2. Living faith is the faith by which we are to live our daily lives in God's kingdom (*Romans 1:17*). It is no different from the faith by which we came into the kingdom of God. The same heart attitudes of repentance and faith in Jesus Christ are to continue all our life.

By faith we read the scriptures, expecting revelation knowledge from the Holy Spirit as we do so. By faith we pray, knowing that there is a loving Father "on the other end of the line" who hears and answers us. By faith we use the gifts of the Spirit, and minister to others. The Christian life is a life of faith from start to finish because it is about our relationship of love and obedience with the unseen Lord of creation. You have this faith too. No doubt you feel that you could use more of it (we'll come to that later), but right now be encouraged: **you are a man/woman of faith!**

Some commentators also distinguish between 'living faith' and 'the gift of faith', whilst others speak of 'the faith of Jesus', or 'the faith of God' as categories distinct from justifying and living faith. Right now let us establish that biblical faith is essentially simple and uncomplicated. Certainly there are aspects of it which are controversial, but these are not central to living the victorious Christian life.

The dynamic faith by which we are to live depends upon what we believe about God. The foundation of our faith is therefore those truths about himself that God has revealed in scripture. Hence, the NT writers talk about 'the Faith'.

3. The Faith.

'The Faith' is the collective term used to describe what we believe about God. There is a body of doctrine (the word 'doctrine' means 'teaching') so fundamental and indispensable to the practice of true Christianity as to actually define it. This is *the faith once delivered to the saints (Jude v3)*. These doctrines are neither optional nor negotiable. NT writers repeatedly stress the necessity of keeping doctrines pure, and also of not having fellowship with those who deny them.

But even if we or an angel from heaven should preach a gospel other than the one we preached to you, let him be eternally condemned! As we have already said, so now I say again: If anybody is accepted, let him be eternally condemned! (Galatians 1:8-9)

...there will be false teachers among you. They will secretly introduce destructive heresies, even denying the sovereign Lord who bought them - bringing swift destruction on themselves. (2 Peter 2:1)

Anyone who runs ahead and does not continue in the teaching of Christ does not have God; whoever continues in the teaching has both the Father and the Son. If anyone comes to you and does not bring this teaching, do not take him into your house or welcome him. Anyone who welcomes him shares in his wicked work. (2 John 1:9-11)

These instructions were written because, even at that very early stage in Church history, false teachers were already corrupting the Apostles' doctrine. The importance of maintaining pure doctrine in the Church was never greater than it is today, because Jesus warned that in the last days of this age even the elect are in danger of being deceived (*Matthew 24:24*).

'Doctrinal faith', or simply 'the Faith', is not dry academic stuff suitable only for those with intellectual leanings.

It is the very foundation of the faith by which we are to live. Thus, unless we believe that God is love, we shall not believe in his love for us personally. If we are not convinced that *in all things God works for the good of those who love him (Romans 8:28)* we may lose our faith under the strain of unexpected trials. **Doctrinal faith is the foundation of living faith.**

Down the centuries many 'creeds' (from the Latin *credo* = I believe) have been constructed as summaries of 'the Faith'. The Apostles' creed (given below), and the Nicene creed, are perhaps the most widely known, but there are also Protestant, Roman Catholic, Greek and Russian creeds. Historically, almost all creeds were written to counteract contemporary error, and are usually inadequate in some respects as balanced summaries of 'The Faith'.

Any list of doctrines fundamental to 'The Faith' must include: (1) justification by faith alone; (2) the absolute authority of scripture over tradition; (3) the deity of Christ, and his bodily resurrection; (4) the Trinity. Such are the test of orthodoxy at which the righteous rejoice and sects stumble and fall. Items (1) & (2) were the issues at the heart of the 16th century Reformation in which Martin Luther figured prominently. They remain the key issues which divide Protestants from Catholics to this day.

In respect of (2) the issue is over the *sufficiency* of scripture, not over its infallibility which is not in question. In other words, the Protestant position is that scripture alone constitutes the word of God which is to be believed. Roman Catholicism flatly rejects this, claiming that the word of God encompasses not only the Bible but also the Apocrypha, the Church's authority to teach and interpret scripture, the Pope's *ex cathedra* pronouncements (which since 1870 are deemed to be infallible), and an ill-defined body of church law and tradition. In effect, this places the authority of the Roman Catholic church above that of scripture.

Concerning (1), justification by faith alone, MacArthur[5] writes: "On the matter of justification the difference between the Roman Catholic view and that of Protestant evangelicalism is so profound as to constitute two wholly different religions. If one view represents authentic Christianity, the other certainly cannot." To Luther, the doctrine of justification by faith alone, and not of faith plus works, was the test of authentic Christianity, and the article by which the church stands or falls.

The Apostles' Creed

I believe in God, the Father almighty,
creator of heaven and earth.

I believe in Jesus Christ, his only Son, our Lord.
He was conceived by the power of the Holy Spirit
and born of the Virgin Mary.
He suffered under Pontius Pilate, was crucified,
died and was buried.
He descended to the dead. On the third day he rose again.
He ascended into heaven, and is seated at the
right hand of the Father.
He will come again to judge the living and the dead.

I believe in the Holy Spirit,
the holy catholic (universal) Church,
the communion of saints, the forgiveness of sins,
the resurrection of the body, and the life everlasting.

Faith and believing.

This next section may seem a little technical and academic but it's the key to a proper understanding of faith and will save us from much woolly thinking and a good deal of mental anguish. The words 'faith' and 'believe' come from the same Greek root and are intimately connected. Nevertheless, the NT usually makes a distinction between them by the context in which they are used. A hint of the importance of such a distinction is afforded by the observation that in his gospel the Apostle John never once used the word 'faith', preferring to use 'believe' exclusively.

'Faith' is a noun, and a noun is a type of word which describes a person, place or thing. 'Believe' is a verb, the type of word which gives action to a noun. Thus: 'ball' is a noun, whereas 'throw' is a verb which tells us what is happening to or with the ball/noun. It's the same with 'faith' and 'believe'.

Faith is formed in us as a response to God's word of truth: *Faith comes from hearing the message, and the message is heard through the word of Christ. (Romans 10:17).* Our response to his initiative is to choose to believe and accept, or to disbelieve and reject. His part is to generate faith in us by his word; our part is to choose to believe what he says and accept what he offers.

This understanding is liberating because the responsibility for generating great faith in us is seen to be his, not ours. What a relief! But what part are we to play in all this? **Only believe!** *(Mark 5:36)*

*To all who received him, to those who **believed** in his name, he gave the right to become children of God. (John 1:12)*

*Then they asked him, "**What must we do** to do the works God requires?" Jesus answered, "The work of God is this: to **believe** in the one he has sent." (John 6:28-29)*

*Simon Peter answered him, "Lord, to whom shall we go? You have the words of eternal life. We **believe** and know that you are the Holy One of God." (John 6:68-69)*

*All the prophets testify about him that everyone who **believes** in him receives forgiveness of sins through his name." (Acts 10:43)*

*I am not ashamed of the gospel, because it is the power of God for the salvation of everyone who **believes**: first for the Jew, then for the Gentile. (Romans 1:16)*

*But what does it say? "The word is near you; it is in your mouth and in your heart," that is, the word of faith we are proclaiming: That if you confess with your mouth, "Jesus is Lord," and **believe** in your heart that God raised him from the dead, you will be saved. For it is with your heart that you **believe** and are justified, and it is with your mouth that you confess and are saved. (Romans 10:8-10)*

*This is his command: to **believe** in the name of his Son, Jesus Christ. (1 John 3:23)*

The consequence of a person believing *in the name of his Son, Jesus Christ* is that *God lives in him and he in God (1John 4:15). Hallelujah!*

By the time John wrote his gospel (generally dated about AD 85) he was an old man. He must have dealt with very many Christians who had problems with faith, and had seen that their confusion was the result of not appreciating what is God's work and what is ours. He therefore decided that he would write about faith using only the verb 'believe', thereby making our part clear. The same distinction is made by the anonymous writer of Hebrews:

And without faith it is impossible to please God, because anyone who comes to him must believe that he exists and that he rewards those who earnestly seek him. (Hebrews 11:6)

We conclude that the NT teaches that to believe is the response of faith which God desires from us. God is the source of our faith in that it is generated in us through his word. "It is our believing that releases faith and brings us into obedience to what God has said." (Judson Cornwall)

*Then he said to Thomas, "Reach your finger here, and look at my hands; and reach your hand here, and put it into my side. Do not be unbelieving but **believe**." And Thomas answered and said to him, "My Lord and my God!'Jesus said to him,"Thomas because you have seen me, you have **believed**. Blessed are those who have not seen and yet have **believed**." (John 20:27-29)*

*But what does it say? "The word is near you; it is in your mouth and in your heart," that is, the word of faith we are proclaiming: That if you confess with your mouth, "Jesus is Lord," and **believe** in your heart that God raised him from the dead, you will be saved. For it is with your heart that you **believe** and are justified, and it is with your mouth that you confess and are saved. (Romans 10:8-10)*

"Faith is the ability to believe." (Dave Duell)[6]

"Belief is mental, while faith is from God."
(Kathryn Kuhlman)[7]

CHAPTER 2

Three Essential Components of Faith

Preview. The three primary components of faith - knowledge, trust and action - are introduced and explained. The relationships of faith to hope, and to love, are exposed.

Introduction.

True biblical faith has three components: knowledge, trust and action. The knowledge is of what God has said; the trust is in God himself; and the action is our response. We look at these three aspects in turn.

"Faith is that act of mind and spirit by which we accept and then act upon the word of God."

1. Faith and knowledge.

Faith comes from hearing the message, and the message is heard through the word of Christ. (Romans 10:17)

"Faith is a conviction based upon knowledge." (W.E. Vine)[1]

Biblical faith is always based upon a word from God. To appreciate the full meaning of this remark we need to know that whereas in English we have only one word called 'word', in the Greek NT two different words are used: both are translated into English as 'word'. They are: *logos* and *rhema*. Both are derived from roots meaning 'to say' and indeed are sometimes translated as 'saying'. *Logos* is used more frequently (>300 times) than *rhema*(70). In the OT the phrase 'the word of the Lord' occurs nearly 400 times, and means simply any communication from God to men, especially through a prophet. Thus, Jeremiah uses the phrase more than 50 times. The same phraseology is found in NT, with both *logos* and *rhema* involved.

Logos means both 'word' and the thought or reason expressed by the words. The whole Bible is the *logos* of God. In John's prologue, however, *logos* is given a unique content: he identifies it with the eternal Son of God, Jesus Christ.

In the beginning was the logos, and the logos was with God and the logos was God. (John 1:1)

In contrast, *rhema* is used of a specific and particular word of God, given for a specific situation. Thus:

*... the sword of the Spirit, which is the word (**rhema**) of God. (Ephesians 6:17)*

Here Paul is talking of the weapons available to us for spiritual warfare. The one offensive weapon is compared to a sword, the sword of the Spirit. It is the individual scripture which the Spirit brings to mind for use in a specific time of need. Jesus' invitation to Peter to walk on water was a *rhema* word to Peter: it is not a *logos* and therefore does not mean that anyone else has the authority to walk on water.

In the Parable of the Sower *(Luke 8)* the seed is identified by Jesus with the logos of God. But in his reply to the Devil, Jesus declared that *man does not live by bread alone, but by every* ***rhema*** *that comes from the mouth of the Lord;* and Jesus' own battle with the Devil *(Luke 4:1-12)* showed that the Father gave him a specific and different *(rhema)* word in answer to each temptation.

With this as background, we can now appreciate the impact of Paul's statement in *Romans 10:17.*

Faith comes from hearing the message,
and the message is heard through a rhema of Christ.

In other words, God inspires faith in you by specific, particular words of truth. Again and again throughout your daily walk with him, especially as you read and dwell in the word, the Bible, he'll speak his words of truth into your being, thereby building you up in knowledge and faith. Faith is your response to what God has already done. It is not what you must do to make God act on your behalf!

He chose to give us birth through the word of truth, that we might be a kind of first fruits of all he created. (James 1:18)

"Faith wakes at the voice of truth and responds to no other sound." (A.W. Tozer)[2]

"Appropriating faith cannot go beyond one's knowledge of the revealed will of God"
"Until we know what God's will is, there is nothing to base our faith on."
(F.F. Bosworth)[3]

"Spiritual discernment begins with God's word.
Authentic faith cannot bypass the mind. It requires that
we engage our intellect as well." (J.F. MacArthur)[4]

In contrast, in scripture, lack of spiritual knowledge is
death. Thus:

*My people are destroyed from lack of knowledge. "Because you
have rejected knowledge, I also reject you as my priests;
because you have ignored the law of your God, I also will
ignore your children.' (Hosea 4:6)*

*The mind of sinful man is death, but the mind controlled by the
Spirit is life and peace; (Romans 8:6)*

2. Faith and trust.

All healthy relationships involve trust. Trust lies at the
heart of marriage, friendships, business, and international
agreements. Thus, it could hardly be otherwise than that trust
should lie at the very heart of our relationship with our creator.
We see that faith, of which trust is a component, is not a
capricious condition that God has chosen as the basis of
salvation, but a reflection of that fundamental ingredient of trust
which must characterise this most awesome and satisfying of
personal relationships. Trust is also the most fragile of
commodities. Once broken, it is hard to restore.

Lack of trust lay at the root of Adam and Eve's sin. They
preferred to trust their own wisdom rather than God's.

Trust in God is the opposite of self-reliance. We rely
wholly upon his free grace for salvation, and not on any
supposed merit of our own. Thus, Paul in analysing Abraham's
faith noted that *the promise comes by faith, so that it may be by grace
(Romans 4:16)*. This understanding of saving faith lay at the
heart of the sixteenth century Reformation. Martin Luther and

the reformers insisted on the biblical position, that justification comes by faith *alone* (Latin: *sola fide*), and not through faith plus some works or merit of our own. The root meaning of the word 'faith' (Greek: *pistis*) is 'trust'.

Our faith (trust, confidence) is in God himself because his character is utterly trustworthy, and in the name of Jesus, which is an expression of his character.

By faith in the name of Jesus, this man whom you see and know was made strong. It is Jesus' name and the faith that comes through him that has given this complete healing to him, as you can all see. (Acts 3:16)

And this is his command: to believe in the name of his Son, Jesus Christ, and to love one another as he commanded us. (1 John 3:23)

Our faith is in God himself, and in the name of Jesus.

[The KJV and, surprisingly also the NIV, renders Romans 3:25 as *...through faith in his blood ...* The NRSV corrects this to *... atonement by his blood, effective through faith ...* Our faith is in the Giver, not the gift, in the living Christ, not in his death. We also note that Christ alone may apply the blood. The church and the individual believer do not have authority to use the blood. By the blood of Christ our 'old man' was put to death with him. Through the Holy Spirit we were raised with him to eternal life, and given authority to use the name (but not the blood) of Jesus.]

The very nature of God's personality is encapsulated in his revelation to Moses at Mount Sinai:

He passed in front of Moses, proclaiming, "The Lord, the Lord, the compassionate and gracious God, slow to anger, abounding in love and faithfulness, maintaining love to thousands, and forgivingwickedness, rebellion and sin." (Exodus 34:6-7).

The unanimous witness of all who have had dealings

with God is that he keeps his word. He is utterly reliable, totally faithful, and he doesn't change his mind.

God is not a man, that he should lie, nor a son of man, that he should change his mind. Does he speak and then not act? Does he promise and not fulfil? (Numbers 23:19)

Your love, O Lord, reaches to the heavens, your faithfulness to the skies. (Psalm 36:5)

God, who has called you into fellowship with his Son Jesus Christ our Lord, is faithful. (1 Corinthians 1:9)

God's faithfulness is an expression of his mercy, his covenant love. Therefore, Jeremiah found this truth boiling up out of his troubled spirit:

Because of the Lord's great mercy we are not consumed, for his compassions never fail. They are new every morning; great is your faithfulness. (Lamentations 3:22-23)

It is important to understand that **God's faithfulness is to his word**. He has bound himself to us by means of covenant promises. All true followers of Christ come within the new covenant of his blood, a covenant made between the Father and his beloved Son on our behalf. It cannot fai*l*.

I will not violate my covenant or alter what my lips have uttered. (Psalm 89:34)

The LORD is faithful to all his promises. (Psalm 145:13)

What I have said, that will I bring about; what I have planned,that will I do. (Isaiah 46:11) Whatever I say will be fulfilled, declares the Sovereign Lord. (Ezekiel 12:28)

Our security lies in knowledge of God's faithfulness (*His faithfulness will be your shield and rampart. Psalm 91:4);* and that brings peace of heart and mind. "All faith ultimately rests on character" (Selwyn Hughes)[5]. Specifically, our faith in God rests upon what he has revealed about himself, that is upon his character.

Faith is a relationship.

We may analyse faith, identify its components, ask how it works and relates to other qualities, but at heart biblical faith is a relationship. Its about my relationship of love and trust with my heavenly Father. Whilst it is important to have a crisp understanding of faith, and of how it works, at the end of the day its not a formula to be used, but a relationship to revel in.

"Faith is trusting God in the face of every fear, every doubt, and every difficulty." (Selwyn Hughes)[6]

"Want of trust is at the root of almost all our sins and all our weaknesses."
(James Hudson Taylor, founder of the China Inland Mission)[7]

"Faith is the one human attribute that is the opposite of depending upon oneself, for it involves trust in or dependence upon another." (Wayne Grudem)[8]

"In essence faith is very simple. It does not ask us to do what God says he will do, only to trust him to do it."
(John McKay)[9]

"A Christian who fails to trust God will tend to live on a diet of fingernails rather than on a diet of faith." (Anon.)

3. Faith and action.

When God has spoken he is to be believed and obeyed.

Thus, faith involves action on the basis of knowledge of what God has said, and the trustworthiness of his character by which we are assured that he will be true to his word. Unless action is added to belief, faith is stillborn.

> *Faith by itself, if it is not accompanied by action, is dead.*
> *But someone will say, "You have faith; I have deeds."*
> *Show me your faith without deeds, and I will show you*
> *my faith by what I do. (James 2:17-18)*

As an example of stillborn faith James reminds his readers *(2:19)* that even demons believe in God, and shudder in terror at the fate that awaits them. Theirs is a faith unaccompanied by action.

Speaking of Abraham, James explains that *his faith was made complete by what he did (James 2:22)*. In *Hebrews 11*, the most extended teaching in scripture on faith, there is paraded one instance after another of the action by which saints proved the genuineness of their faith. By faith Noah built an ark; Abraham and Sarah had a child in extreme old age; the Israelis walked across the bed of the Red Sea; and many others, known and unknown, pleased God. It is by faith that we are *sure of what we hope for and certain of what we do not see (Hebrews 11:1)*, and therefore are not afraid to step out in the corresponding action. Paul, likewise, talks of the *obedience that comes from faith (Romans 1:5)*.

> *By faith Noah, when warned about things not yet seen, in holy fear built an ark to save his family. (Hebrews 11:7)*

Jesus said: *He who is not with me is against me (Matthew 12:30)*. You can be 'with' him in principle, but unless you obey him and act on what he has said, you are against him, because to disobey is to be opposed to him. Jesus also said: *Whoever is not against us is for us (Mark 9:40)*. That is, those who are not against him, either actively or passively, are 'for' him, as is shown by the evidence of their good works.

Do not merely listen to the word, and so deceive yourselves.
Do what it says. (James 1:22)

"Faith comes by hearing, but it operates by speaking."
(Colin Urquhart)

"Faith is not something we think or say, but something
we do." (David Pawson)[10]

"Everything we receive from God comes to us in spiritual
form. It is the job of faith to get it into physical form."
(Andrew Wommack)

Faith and obedience.
"Obedience is of the very essence of faith." (Andrew
Murray)[11]

Faith, obedience and love are very closely related in
scripture. Our love of God is expressed by our obedience: *If you*
love me you will obey what I command (John 14:15). In *A Theological*
Word Book of the Bible we find that:

"In the OT the word 'obey' is used to bring out the full meaning
of the verb 'to hear'. It indicates the right response to 'the voice'
or 'the word' of God. To hear is to be persuaded and so to obey."
Moreover, "The word 'obey' and its associates are used in the
closest possible association with 'believe' and its associates. The
actions denoted by these two groups of words are almost
indistinguishable."[12]

"Faith is of the heart, invisible to men; obedience is of the
conduct and may be observed. When a man obeys God he gives
the only possible evidence that in his heart he believes God."[13]

This is faith expressing itself in obedience to God. Since
obedience is itself the proof of our love of God, it follows that

we may speak of faith expressing itself in love, as did Paul *(Galatians 5:6)*. Obedience is the response of love and is therefore an end in itself, not a means to an end. "Under the new covenant 'obedient' becomes almost a technical term for those who are joined to Christ."[12] Indeed, Peter writes of those:

> ....*who have been chosen according to the foreknowledge of God the Father, through the sanctifying work of the Spirit, for obedience to Jesus Christ and sprinkling by his blood.*
> *(1 Peter 1:2)*

and John: *"Those who obey his commands live in him, and he in them (1 John 3:24).*

"Faith is following God's initiative." (Colin Urquhart)

Obedience results in glory.

Jesus obeyed his Father, completed the work given to him, and thereby brought glory to the Father. Likewise, the disciples through their obedience to Jesus brought glory to Jesus. So do we as we act in obedience to Jesus' commands. Obedience, *the obedience that comes from faith*, results in glory.

> *I have brought you glory on earth by completing the work you gave me to do. (John 17:4)*

> *Glory has come to me through them (the disciples). (John 17:10)*

We know from the prophets that before the return of Christ great glory will be released upon earth. This will be the glory of Christ resulting from the obedience of the end-time church.

> *For the earth will be filled with the knowledge of the glory of the LORD, as the waters cover the sea. (Habakkuk 2:14)*

Faith and hope.

Faith is being sure of what we hope for and certain of what we do not see (Hebrews 11:1). The word 'hope' has a specific meaning in the NT. Whereas in common usage it usually includes elements of doubt (e.g. "I hope the bus will come!") and of natural desire, in the NT 'hope' implies a "favourable and confident expectation" based upon a word of God. "It has to do with the unseen and the future"[14]. Hope is the bridge between the *rhema* word which arouses faith, and its eventual manifestation.

> *Hope that is seen is no hope at all. Who hopes for what he already has? But if we hope for what we do not yet have, we wait for it patiently. (Romans 8:24-25)*

Faith	Hope
Established in the present Primarily in the heart	Directed towards the future Primarily in the mind.

In the NT the word 'hope' is used in two main senses. Commonly it refers to the object of our hope, that is Christ and all that his return at the end of the age implies: *Christ Jesus our hope (1 Timothy 1:1); Christ in you the hope of glory (Colossians 1:27),* etc. We focus here on the subjective use of 'hope', that is, the attitude of hoping. To live in hope is to walk by faith as opposed to sight.

Biblical hope is, thus, inseparable from faith in God: the one cannot exist without the other. Indeed, the God who strikes faith in our hearts is also *the God of hope who is able to fill us with all joy and peace .. so that you may overflow with hope by the power of the Holy Spirit (Romans 15:13).*

Hope, the hope of salvation *(1 Thessalonians 5:8)*, is both part of our defensive armour; and *an anchor for the soul, firm and secure (Hebrews 6:19)*, rooted in the reality of our intimacy with God and our trust of him.

"Hope is the daughter of faith." (Andrew Murray)[15]

When God spoke to Abraham *(Genesis 12:1-3)* there was both a command and a promise, which illuminated the reason for the command. Abraham obeyed the command and moved home. He also accepted the promise and responded correctly by entertaining the hope that the promised blessings would follow.

God spoke again to Abraham *(Genesis 15:1-8)*, confirming the promise of descendants from his own body and blood. Given the ages of Abraham and his wife this seemed unlikely in the extreme, but Paul tells us that Abraham's faith was in:

God who gives life to the dead and calls things that are not as though they were. Against all hope, Abraham in hope believed, and so became the father of many nations.
(Romans 4:17-18)

The phrase *in hope* shows that Abraham at that time had both faith and hope: hope concerning the future and faith in the present. And this hope for the future was the product of his faith in God in the present. Thus, Abraham turned a deaf ear to the evidence of his senses, choosing to believe God's *rhema* word to him, and so by faith he saw the unseen.

For us, as for Abraham, our faith is in God, our hope is in his promises to us.

God speaks by way of:	command	promise
Our response:	obedience	hope

May the God of hope fill you with all joy and peace as you trust in him, so that you may overflow with hope by the power of the Holy Spirit. (Romans 15:13)

I have put my hope in your word. (Psalm 119:74)

> "What'er we hope, by faith we have
> Future and past subsisting now."
> (From a hymn by Charles Wesley)[16]

Faith and love.

In his letters Paul talks quite often of the link between faith and love. Interestingly, Jesus never did. Of course, Jesus talked about love, but he stressed the link with obedience rather than with faith. *If anyone loves me, he will obey my teaching (John 14:21,23).* In fact, he made twice as many references to love as to faith.

Jesus taught that the greatest commandments are: to love God, and to love your neighbour as yourself *(Mark 12:28-32)*. Naturally, Paul, who had received his gospel directly from Christ by supernatural revelation *(Galatians 1:11-12)*, taught the same. In fact he identified love as one of the three qualities, together with faith and hope, which are eternal in nature, love being the greatest *(1 Corinthians 13:13)*. The Psalmist also understood the connection between faith (trust) and love: *The Lord's unfailing love surrounds the man who trusts in him. (Psalm 32:10).*

We choose to obey God out of love for him, and because our personal experience of him consistently reaffirms his character as revealed in scripture. Therefore we should always be ready to do what he says, to move into action in response to his *logos* and *rhema* words to us. This is faith in operation, motivated by love. And that's what Paul said:

The only thing that counts is faith expressing itself through love. (Galatians 5:6)

Note, however, that it is faith which produces love, not love which generates faith, because we must first believe in his love before we can respond to it.

In the gospel records of Jesus' ministry it is noted repeatedly that he acted out of compassion in his teaching and healing. The same Spirit of Jesus is in us, the same anointing and therefore the same fountain of compassion, because it is the Holy Spirit who pours this love of God into our hearts *(Romans 5:5)*. Love is the driving force which triggers faith into action for making Jesus known, for healing, and for godly servanthood.

"You and I will never do anything except on the line of compassion. We shall never be able to remove the cancer until we are immersed so deeply in the power of the Holy Spirit that the compassion of Christ is moving through us." (Smith Wigglesworth)[17]

Again: *The only thing that counts is faith expressing itself through love. (Galatians 5:6)*

Like faith, love involves action - it must be expressed in some way. Obedience is the response God requires of us to his word of command, and we are ready to obey because we love him. Thus, the resulting action is, at one and the same time, the proof of our love, and a necessary component of the faith by which we fulfil the command. Love and faith are inseparable: both are heart responses. Moreover, since they are *the faith and love that are in Christ Jesus (1 Timothy 1:14)* they are eternal in quality, and hope travels with them because it is simply that attitude of heart and mind which is confident of the outcome. Therefore these three remain: faith, hope and love. *But the greatest of these is love. (1 Corinthians 13:13).*

> *Hope does not disappoint us, because God has poured out his love into our hearts by the Holy Spirit, whom he has given us. (Romans 5:5)*

> *We continually remember before our God and Father your work produced by faith, your labor prompted by love, and your endurance inspired by hope in our Lord Jesus Christ. (1 Thessalonians 1:3)*

"Love gives faith hands and feet; hope lends it wings. Love is the fire at its heart and the lifeblood coursing in its veins, while hope is the light that gleams and dances in its eyes. (Judson Cornwall)[18]

Faith and certainty.

When you have heard from God, through the scriptures brought alive to you by the Holy Spirit, or directly by his word into your spirit, you know that you know that he has spoken. There is no doubt about it. Thus, the writer of Hebrews defined faith:

> *Faith is being sure of what we hope for and certain of what we do not see. (Hebrews 11:1)*

Faith has no question marks. It's about being sure and certain. You have faith only for what you are sure and certain of. Faith knows what will happen. Thus, *Hebrews 11:1* is a precise and highly restrictive definition of faith. Much of what passes for faith in the church today is not. This definition focusses us on God himself and makes us utterly dependent upon him, because unless and until God has spoken into our situation, we have nothing upon which to base our faith.

Finally ...

Faith is a condition of the heart, not the mind alone. It is in the present, not the future. Faith is not based upon the evidence of our physical senses, but on the invisible eternal truths brought to us by God's *logos* and *rhema* word. It accepts the evidence of the senses only when this agrees with God's word. In spiritual matters sight follows faith. The world says: "Seeing is believing", but the man of faith responds: "Believing is seeing".

The Jesus said, "Did I not tell you that if you believed,
you would see the glory of God? (John 11:40)

Faith is ... the evidence of things not seen. (Hebrews 11:1 KJV)

We live by faith, not by sight. (2 Corinthians 5:7)

"Genuine faith can no more manifest itself without result than the sun can shine without light and heat." (Charles Price)

CHAPTER 3

All the Negatives

Preview. The negative factors of fear, unbelief, doubt and presumption are defined and contrasted. A simple pictorial model of faith is introduced and used to deduce possible hindrances to faith.

Faith, fear and unbelief.

Jesus contrasted faith and fear on several occasions. Thus, to Jairus: *Don't be afraid; just believe and she will be healed (Luke 8:50).* To the disciples afraid of sinking in a storm on Galilee: *Why are you so afraid? Do you still have no faith? (Mark 4:40).* Moreover, we have seen that faith and love work together, and we know also that *there is no fear in love (1 John 4:18)*. Thus, the opposite of faith is fear.

Where faith says: "It shall be", fear says: "It can't be".

"Fear looks but faith jumps." (Smith Wigglesworth)

Closely allied to fear are doubt and unbelief. The Greek word for faith is *pistis*. In Greek prefixing a word with 'a' makes it into the negative form, as in *apistia*. *Apistia* is translated as unbelief or, sometimes, as 'lack of faith'. Unbelief is the absence of faith, rather than its opposite - which is fear. Similar shades of meaning apply to a word such as 'moral':

Noun	Verb	Adjective
Pistis = faith, belief	*Pisteuo* = to believe	*Pistos* = believing, *trusting*
Apistia = *unbelief*	*Apisteo* = to disbelieve	*Apistos* = unbelieving
Faith	Unbelief	Fear
Moral	Amoral	Immoral

A hint of the seriousness of unbelief is had from the observation that about half of Jesus' references to faith are to the lack of it. Paul wrote that *it is with the heart that you believe and are justified (Romans 10:9)*. Therefore, unbelief shows that there is something wrong with the heart. It is not simply an intellectual problem. God speaks to the heart, and looks for openness, love and faith in it.

Faith is based on a word spoken by God. To believe that word, and to act on it, is faith. Unbelief is a refusal to believe that word of God. In scripture such an attitude is called 'hardness of heart'. Hardness of heart is a choice to believe and act upon something other than God's word spoken into the situation. Thus, the cause of unbelief is not the unavailability of faith, but refusal to allow that faith to function. It is a choice, and therefore also a sin, *because everything that does not come from faith is sin (Romans 14:23).*

See to it, brothers, that none of you has a sinful, unbelieving heart that turns away from the living God. (Hebrews 3:12)

Anyone, then, who knows the right thing to do and fails to do it, commits sin. (James 4:17 NRSV).

"Unbelief is the darkroom in which our negatives are developed." (Andrew Wommack)

"Unbelief is believing in the flesh, not the Spirit." (Colin Urquhart)

"Unbelief is treating God with contempt." (Colin Urquhart)

"Unbelief is not a can't, its a won't." (Anon)

Faith and unbelief can co-exist, and probably do so in all of us. Recall the heartfelt plea of the anxious parent in *Mark 9:24:*

Immediately the boy's father exclaimed, "I do believe; help me overcome my unbelief!"

To treat unbelief it is necessary to uncover the root cause of the refusal to trust the known word of God and to act upon it. In this, the gifts of the Spirit, especially the word of knowledge, are essential.

"The difference between the unbeliever and the believer is this: the one is a man of the world, and lives here; the other is a man of God, and lives in heaven." (Andrew Murray)[1]

Fear, on the other hand, arises from ignorance of God's word, coupled with lack of understanding of it, and lack of trust in God. Indeed, the basis of all fear is lack of trust. The fearful need to be assured of the love of God for them, and surrounded by his love expressed through the church, because there is no fear in love. Sometimes it may be necessary to command a spirit of fear to go, but more commonly fear is to be treated by application of the word of God, combined with loving support and encouragement to put that word into action. Thereby, faith develops through love and, according to the apostle Paul, that's what matters.

> *There is no fear in love. But perfect love drives out fear, because fear has to do with punishment. The one who fears is not made perfect in love. (1 John 4:18)*

Faith and doubt. (Based upon *Doubt* by Os Guinness)[2]
The distinction between doubt and unbelief is crucial. "Doubt is a state of mind in suspension between faith and unbelief": it has elements of both. The root meaning of the word 'doubt' is 'two'. All five Greek NT words which are translated as 'doubt' reflect some aspect of this duality of mind and heart. A person is torn between two opinions, unable to make up his mind, debating with himself, or weighing up his options. He is 'in two minds'. Both heart and mind are divided. Doubt is literally "faith in two minds".

> *Elijah went before the people and said, "How long will you waver between two opinions? If the LORD is God, follow him; but if Baal is God, follow him." (1 Kings 18:21)*
>
> *I hate double-minded men, but I love your law. (Psalm 119:113)*
>
> *When he asks, he must believe and not doubt, because he who doubts is like a wave of the sea, blown and tossed by the wind. That man should not think he will receive anything from the Lord. (James 1:6-7)*

Purify your hearts, you who are double-minded (James 4:8)

Three basic misconceptions about doubt.

1. That doubt is wrong and is effectively the same thing as unbelief. The above definitions of doubt and unbelief show that this is not true. Nevertheless, in some circles faith is pictured as the absence of doubt - and that is tantamount to spiritual repression. To insist that to be genuine faith must be doubt-free is more destructive of genuine faith than the worst doubts. What destroys faith is not doubt but the disobedience that hardens into unbelief.

2. That doubt is something to be ashamed of because it is dishonest to say that you believe if you have doubts. In fact the seriousness with which a person treats their doubts is a measure of how seriously and honestly they treat their faith. Doubt should always be taken seriously.

Faith is always tested - in order to reveal how much of it is real and firmly based upon the rock which is Christ. Not infrequently we find ourselves asking: 'God, is that really you, or am I imagining it?' Is this what your word really says about this or that? Can I really trust God in every area of my life? The great men of faith reached the heights only by facing their doubts, by going through the depths.

3. That doubt is a problem of faith but not of knowledge. All true faith depends upon knowledge of the object of that faith. Knowledge and faith are inseparable. In fact, in order to know anything we must assume certain things in faith. It is often suggested that faith begins where knowledge ends: that is not true. If faith does not begin, neither will reason and knowledge. The largest part of doubting comes from ignorance of what God has said.

"Doubt is faith suffering from mistreatment or malnutrition."
(Os Guinness)

"When you feed your faith, you starve your doubts."
(Lester Sumrall)

"Doubt is a promise-killer, but faith in God leads
to fulfilment." (R. Bonnke)

Finally ....

doubt is normal - but it should only be temporary and should always be resolved. That way, faith is confirmed, not denied. To the Christian doubt is useful in exposing what should not be believed. Therefore, let us be open about our doubts.

Resolving doubts. How may doubt be resolved? Go back to the word of God. Work forward from there. And talk with those who are mature in the faith. Those who face doubts honestly are the ones who go on to be overcomers. Its better to doubt and resolve your doubts, than to find in the day of testing that you are standing on sand, not rock.

"Honest doubt is healthy. Cynical doubt is damaging and
self-destructive." (Selwyn Highes)[3]

Be merciful to those who doubt. (Jude v22)

Faith and presumption.

Faith is a response to God's initiative, his *logos* or *rhema* word spoken into a situation. In contrast, presumption lacks a word from the Lord. In it the believer takes the initiative, acting in independence of God. The results are always disappointing because, unless God has spoken, nothing will happen. The incident recorded in *Numbers 14* (*v44* especially) is classical of presumption.

Who can speak and have it happen if the Lord has not decreed it? (Lamentations 3:37)

Jesus must have been many times by the Pool of Bethesda

in Jerusalem, and the cripple he healed *(John 5:2ff)* had been a fixture there for years, but Jesus waited until on a specific day the Father said: "Heal him". Certainly, God heals but the timing and the manner must also be his.

The key issue is: what has God said? Sometimes we may fail to discern that a thought is in fact from our own flesh, probably the product of our feelings, and not of God. *The heart is deceitful above all things (Jeremiah 17:9).* Therefore, presumption often masquerades as faith. However, we can be sincerely wrong, and there is no condemnation from God if we are, because all of us are on a learning curve. Nevertheless, let us note that particular strictures are applied in scripture to false prophets *(Jeremiah 23:15-40; Galatians 1:6-9).* Let us be cautious about claiming: "Thus says the Lord ... " Better, often, to say: "I believe the Lord is saying .... ".

Presumption may also arise from mistaking a *logos* word of God for a *rhema* word. Yongi Cho tells of three Christian Korean girls who needed to cross a river in flood. The bridge was down but they reasoned that if Peter could walk on water, so could they. They drowned. Jesus' word to Peter whilst on Galilee was a *rhema* word intended only for Peter in that hour.

It is presumption also, to expect a biblical promise to apply to us when we have not met the attached conditions. Thus, the great prayer promise of *John 14:13 (I will do whatever you ask in my name)* was made by Jesus to his disciples, those whose lives were fully committed to him, and not to the crowd. Similarly, it does not apply to the semi-committed and to pew-fillers who are plainly not meeting the condition of submission to Jesus' Lordship (see also p 88ff).

More generally, presumption is liable to affect those who refuse to allow God to be sovereign in their life, those who are insolent, proud or arrogant. Our protection against the errors which lead to presumption lies in humble submission to each other within the body/church.

Hindrances to faith.

Many authors have given lists of hindrances to faith, some of which vary both in number and content. A logical set follows from Figure 3.1 because each node in the diagram represents the possibility of an upset. But first a question. Why are there hindrances to our faith?

Faith releases the power of God, unbelief stops it. Thus, the devil attacks faith in order to frustrate the will of God. Faith is the key to the signs and wonders with which God confirms his word when it is spoken in the power of the Spirit. The devil is against anything that brings glory to God. Therefore, like Paul, we must not be unaware of his schemes *(2 Corinthians 2:11)*.

> "Faith is the normal atmosphere of heaven. By faith the weakest may storm the battlements of Hell. Therefore, all Hell is against it." (Harold Horton)[4]

These hindrances follow from Figure 3.1:

1. Ignorance of God's word and will. Faith cannot be active if we are ignorant of God's will in a given situation. Jesus did and said only what he received from the Father: he hasn't changed his way of doing things, except that he now does it through you and me. It is fundamental to faith and to our whole walk with God that we become and remain students of his word, and that we learn to listen to the Holy Spirit.

2. Satanic lies. Satan opposes God's word with lies, by stealing it, and by subtle suggestions which fuel doubt and unbelief and therefore destroy faith. Satan is a liar and the father of lies. God is truth. Therefore, learn to discern those thoughts which are of the devil: they are always negative, destructive of faith, and contrary to God's word.

3. *Reason*. God gave us minds, intending us to use them to the full. The trouble is that his thoughts and ways are higher than ours *(Isaiah 55:8)* and we sometimes have trouble accepting them. Submit your mind to God and to his word.

"God is not opposed to reason: he is simply beyond reason!"
(Colin Urquhart).

4. *Emotions and feelings*. These are the product of our thinking. Feelings are affected by our perceptions. Only God's truth is both absolute and reliable. You cannot live by feelings - they are likely to change too rapidly. Therefore choose the truth of God's word.

5. *Unwillingness to obey God*. All inputs to our consciousness (God's word, Satan's lies, feelings, reason and circumstances) are channelled through the will. There they await a decision: accept or reject; believe or disbelieve; obey or disobey.

The will is king of the soul. It is where self reigns, procrastination festers, and hardness of heart originates. Renewal of the will is the key issue in Christian discipleship. On the great and terrible 'day of the Lord' every person's will shall be forced to acknowledge the undeniable fact, that Jesus Christ is Lord. Listen to Frank Bartelman, the chief intercessor behind the Los Angeles revival of 1906:

"A place of utter abandonment of will had been reached, in absolute consciousness of helplessness, purified from natural self-activity. This process had been cumulative. ... My mind, the last fortress of man to yield, was taken possession of by the Spirit. The waters that had been gradually accumulating went over my head. I was possessed of him fully. ... Nothing hinders faith and the operation of the Spirit so much as the self-assertiveness of the human soul."

6. *Unwillingness to resolve doubts*. Left to themselves doubts

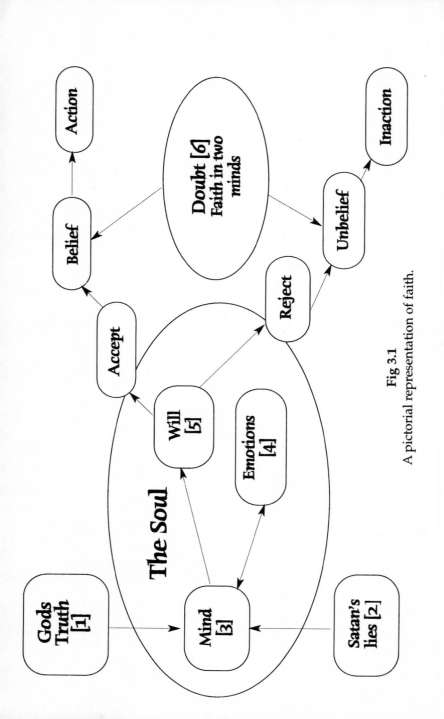

Fig 3.1
A pictorial representation of faith.

harden into unbelief. To leave doubts unresolved is finally a choice for disobedience. Nevertheless, pastorally it may be that deep hurts prevent resolution of doubts unless and until those hurts have been brought to the cross.

7. Inaction. *Faith without works is dead. (James 2:26) Whoever has my commands and obeys them, he is the one who loves me. (John 14:21)* Summed up in Mary's words to the servants at the wedding: *Do whatever he tells you (John 2:5).* As you step out in faith in what he has said, by way of *rhema* or *logos*, his power will accompany you.

Summary.
1. The first four (1 to 4) of these hindrances are related to our handling of scripture and therefore highlight the critical importance of continual input of the word of God. Knowledge of scripture (1) enables us to discern Satan's lies (2) and deal with them. Likewise, bringing our thinking in line with biblical truth channels the emotions and feelings (3) within godly boundaries. It is vital also to submit our thinking and reasoning (4) to God, and to avoid being self-opinionated. As you learn to ask God for his understanding and wisdom, you will experience a glorious flow of revelation.

2. Items 5 to 7 are associated with bringing the will under the Spirit's control. Procrastination, laziness and unbelief may all play a part. The common feature here is disobedience to God.

Any or all of these factors may hinder the operation of faith in us. Reverse them and you have the keys to growing in faith. We return to this matter in the next Chapter.

CHAPTER **4**

Entering Into and Growing in Faith

Preview. This Chapter deals first with the link between faith and repentance. Entry into faith is seen to be, paradoxically, both a gift of God and our free response to his word. The gift of faith is introduced. The crucial issue of growth in faith is then treated. Finally, the place of perseverance is noted.

Faith and repentance.

The NT writers are clear on this point: that repentance must go before faith. Indeed, without true repentance there cannot be true faith. Thus:

John Baptist:
John came, baptising in the desert region and preaching a baptism of repentance for the forgiveness of sins. (Mark 1:4)
Jesus:
"The time has come," he said. "The kingdom of God is near.

Repent and believe the good news! (Mark 1:15)
Luke:
Repentance and forgiveness of sins will be preached in his name to all nations, beginning at Jerusalem. (Luke 24:47)

Peter.
Repent and be baptised, every one of you, in the name of Jesus Christ so that your sins may be forgiven. (Acts 2:38)

Paul:
I have declared to both Jews and Greeks that they must turn to God in repentance and have faith in our Lord Jesus.
(Acts 20:21)

Justifying (or saving) faith involves turning to God, and to turn to God one must first turn from sin. Thus, God demands repentance as the first response to the gospel. Nothing else can take its place. Without true repentance, faith is an empty profession, which is one reason many Christians today are unstable and insecure. They are seeking to build upon a foundation of sand, for their 'faith' is no more than intellectual assent. They have never had a personal encounter with Christ and therefore cannot be truly committed to him. Their 'faith' does not produce any vital change in their lives. Today the message preached is often "only believe", whereas God himself *commands all people everywhere to repent (Acts 17:30).*

Repentance is far more than remorse over sins committed: it is, above all, recognition of a broken relationship. Hence, it is commonly accompanied by godly sorrow, even bitter tears. But because God adds no condemnation, repentance ends in joy, for by it we are restored to that intimate and loving relationship with God for which we were created - and over that all heaven rejoices.

Repentance also involves a willingness to allow God to reorient one's personality and way of thinking. Indeed, the word 'repent' comes from the Greek *metanoia*, which means a change of mind. To repent is, therefore, to re-think, to turn about and travel in the opposite direction. It is the turning from our wicked ways of which *2 Chronicles 7:14* speaks; and the separation from unclean practices recorded in *Ezra 6:21*. Therefore, repentance is far more than asking God to forgive our sin by covering it with the blood of Jesus. It is a deliberate invitation to God to change something in our heart - permanently. Unless the root cause is dealt with, we shall sin repeatedly in the same way and know no freedom from it. It is part of the renewing of the mind *(Romans 12:2)* which is fundamental to our discipleship.

The phrase *acts that lead to death (Hebrews 6:1)* includes everything not based upon faith. Even the activities of professing Christians are 'dead works' if they are not built upon faith, because *everything that does not come from faith is sin (Romans 14:23)*. For this reason Isaiah cries out:

All our righteous acts are like filthy rags. (Isaiah 64:6)

Jesus gave a dramatic case of that: *Luke 13:1-5*. These men died in the very act of performing a religious rite yet, Jesus said, they went to eternal death. Why? Because their act of sacrifice in the temple was not based upon repentance. The same is still true.

Faith and repentance are in action not only at the point of new birth: they are heart attitudes which should continue throughout our lives as Christ's disciples.

"Repentance is a change of mind about where life is found." (Selwyn Hughes)[1]

Repentance is not a condition for going home. It is going home." (Selwyn Hughes)[2]

"Repentance is a return to obedience." (Andrew Murray)[3]

Repentance is a gift of God.

Repentance is both a gift of God, and our uncoerced heart response to God's initiative. It is often the result of an encounter with Christ. The story of Zacchaeus illustrates this beautifully *(Luke 19:1-10)*. Repentance originates in the free, sovereign grace of God. The initiative is always with him, moving the sinner to repentance.

Turn us back to you, O Lord, and we will be restored.
(Lamentations 5:21)

I will give them a heart to know me, that I am the Lord.
(Jeremiah 24:7)

No-one can come to me unless the Father who sent
me draws him. (John 6:44)

God exalted him [Jesus] ... that he might give repentance
and forgiveness of sins to Israel. (Acts 5:31)

The Lord opened her heart to respond to Paul's message. (Acts
16:14)

... God's kindness leads you towards repentance. (Romans 2:4)

Those who oppose him he must gently instruct, in the hope that
God will grant them repentance leading them to a
knowledge of the truth .... (2 Timothy 2:25)

Entering into faith.

In scripture, faith comes in two ways: by hearing and responding to the word of God, and as a gift. How are we to understand this paradox? † How much is down to God and how much to us? Where does the balance lie?

[✝ A paradox, alerts us to the fact that we are dealing, not just with an isolated issue, but with one aspect of a general problem. Christianity is littered with paradoxes: the God who is both One and Three in One; the incarnation ("Our God contracted to a span"); predestination and freewill; to name but three. Paradoxes are warning signs placed by God at the boundaries of the secret with the revealed.

The secret things belong to the LORD our God, but the things revealed belong to us and to our children forever, that we may follow all the words of this law (Deuteronomy 29:29). Why? So that we shall walk by faith and not by sight. God deals with us on a need-to-know basis. He gives all the revelation we need, and then asks that we walk by faith.

It is not that faith takes over where reason fails; it is simply that there are boundaries beyond which we may not penetrate. In this life we must be content to know in part *(1 Corinthians 13:12)* and to live with mystery. This is not an anti-intellectual stance, but a reminder that God has placed boundaries on what we may know of him and his ways.]

Its not a new question: Augustine(354-430) considered it, and the discussion has rattled on down the centuries. Does it matter, then? Can't we just get on with living by faith regardless of how we come by it? Yes, we can, but there are, nevertheless, many urgent warnings in the epistles about the importance of knowing our doctrines and keeping them pure. This is not an academic issue. The Christian faith is under attack from many directions, and we need a clear understanding of the truth in order to defend it.

Paul's statement that *faith comes from hearing the message, and the message is heard through the word of Christ (Romans 10:17)*, falls within the context of a discussion of Israel's lack of response to the gospel. God has spared no effort to bring the word to them, or indeed, to us. The preacher and the word he brings can reasonably be called God's gift. Those who accept, believe and act on the word brought to them, are said to have responded in faith, and to have entered God's kingdom. God's part is to take the initiative and see that we hear the word; our part is to chose to believe what we hear.

Paul also talks explicitly of faith as a gift, as does Peter:

"...think of yourself with sober judgement, in accordance with the measure of faith God has given you. (Romans 12:3)

For it is by grace you have been saved, through faith—and this not from yourselves, it is the gift of God— (Ephesians 2:8)

The grace of our Lord was poured out on me abundantly, along with the faith and love that are in Christ Jesus. (1 Timothy 1:14)

By faith in the name of Jesus, this man whom you see and know was made strong. It is Jesus' name and the faith that comes through him that has given this complete healing to him, as you can all see.
(Acts 3:16)

Faith is a gift, but a gift needs to be received, so although the balance is heavily on God's side in this description, there is still a part in the process played by those who receive it. God will not dump faith into our laps regardless of whether or not we want it, as Paul showed in respect of Israel.

Viewed like this, the two means of acquiring faith are seen to be much closer than appears at first sight. Indeed, it is wrong to view them as separate and distinct. Taken together, the balance tilts strongly towards what God has done for us, and this is surely why in scripture these two expressions of the means of entry into faith are given.

God's persistence in speaking his words of life and healing to his creation is breathtaking. To say only that his part is to speak and ours to believe, is to leave the balance tilted excessively towards us, to leave out of account the passion and determination with which he has pursued each of us down the years until we responded. Viewed in this light, it becomes difficult not to view faith as a gift, the receiving of it being such a small part of the whole.

Our part is, of course, vital in that what God looks for is our individual heart response of trust, love and obedience, but it is better seen as the trigger which releases the deluge of God's grace upon us, rather than a process in which we are co-equal partners with him. Indeed, the closer we draw to God the more evident it becomes how small is our part, and how awesome and gracious is his. Hence, "In revival those who once thought themselves fitted for heaven stand amazed that they are not consigned to hell"[4], and the word upon their lips is not "Lord, we did it together" but "Glory to the Lamb!"

Every good and perfect gift is from above, coming down from the Father of the heavenly lights, who does not change like shifting shadows. He chose to give us birth through the word of truth, that we might be a kind of first fruits of all he created. (James 1:17-18)

" Through him [Christ] you believe in God. 1Peter 1 : 21

Matthew Henry (1662-1714) summed it up beautifully. Commenting on *Romans 10:17*, he wrote: "God gives faith, but it is by the word as the instrument."[5]

"Faith can be received only as it is imparted to our hearts by God himself." (Kathryn Kuhlman)

"We have made faith a condition of the mind
 when it is a divinely imparted grace of the heart."
(Charles S. Price)

The gift of faith.
        We have seen that God gives faith. However, 'the gift of faith' is a separate issue. It is one of the gifts of the Spirit listed in *1 Corinthians 12:9*. This is the sole explicit mention of it in scripture, and the gift is nowhere defined or illustrated. Hence, there are varieties of opinions about it.

        As with all the gifts of the Spirit, 'the gift of faith' is supernatural and can operate only under the Spirit's direction and anointing. Thus, it is called into operation by the Spirit in whatever circumstances he chooses, with the co-operation of the believer. There seems to be no reason to believe that the faith thus released is any different in kind from the faith by which we are saved and then live our lives in obedience to Christ, although some dispute this. What is certain is that the level of it is extraordinary.

        The consensus of present-day thinking is that 'the gift of faith' operates at a specific moment in time, releasing the power of God to perform a supernatural act, such as calming a storm, raising the dead, or healing a profoundly disabled person. Similarly, it may enable a person to believe God for a mighty manifestation, such as a coming revival. More generally, it operates in a believer to pitch him into what is for him a new level of faith action.

"The gift of faith dares in the face of everything. It is as we are in the Spirit that the Spirit of God will operate this gift anywhere and at any time. When the Spirit of God is operating this gift within a man, he causes him to know what God is going to do." (Smith Wigglesworth)[6]

"The gift of faith brings forth a spring of belief from within and propels us to operate in the supernatural realm. It's a present-tense faith, sensing that God will make a special event happen." (Mahesh Chavda)[7]

Oral Roberts describes 'the gift of faith' as "the supernatural removal of doubt and fear", although it would probably be more accurate to speak of the removal of unbelief and fear. Other modern miracle workers report in similar terms. In contemporary language we might say that: 'the gift of faith' is a turbo-charged level of faith which God may kick into action at a point of specific need. It is about Christ-like capability.

In the context of the gift of faith, the faith action required is speaking. God initiates an event by revealing his will through a vision, a word, or simply by an assurance that he is about to act extraordinarily. *Since we have the same spirit of faith as he had who wrote, "I believed, and so I spoke," we too believe, and so we speak (2 Corinthians 4:13 RSV).* With the gift comes a deep peace, and a confidence that what God has said will happen.

The key to operating in the gift of faith is relationship with the Holy Spirit. This in turn involves three essentials: (1) obedience to his voice, (2) brokenness, (3) humility. Only God must have the glory.

"Everyone who wants to do the works of Jesus must develop a living relationship with the Holy Spirit. We begin by taking baby steps of recognising and obeying his voice. As we accomplish simple tasks, he moves us on to greater and greater works." (Mahesh Chavda)[8]

Growing in faith.

We ought always to thank God for you, brothers, and rightly so, because your faith is growing more and more, and the love every one of you has for each other is increasing. (2 Thessalonians 1:3)

Our hope is that, as your faith continues to grow, our area of activity among you will greatly expand. (2 Corinthians 10:15)

What Jesus said.

Jesus wants disciples, a kingdom full of disciples. A disciple understudies the Master with the aim of becoming like him. Jesus is the One who has gone ahead of us demonstrating perfect faith. *He is the author and perfector of our faith (Hebrews 12:2).*

In this text, the Greek word (*archegos*) translated as 'author' means 'one who leads'. The NRSV rendering of it as 'pioneer' catches the meaning precisely. Moreover, the word 'our' "does not correspond to anything in the original and may well be omitted"[9]. Thus, we may render this scripture as: 'Jesus is the pioneer and perfect example of life lived by faith'.

"Christ in the days of his flesh trod undeviatingly the path of faith, and as the Perfector has brought it to a perfect end in his own person."[9]

What this text does not say is that Jesus is the One who both gives faith and brings it to perfection within us. That faith is (in part, at least) a gift of God, and that he expects us to develop in its use, is beyond question, but *Hebrews 12:2* does not deal with these issues. Its purpose is to hold up Jesus as our perfect example of the life of faith, and to encourage us to live like him.

Jesus, then, is the *pioneer and perfector of our faith*

(Hebrews 12:2 NRSV), the One who has gone ahead of us, demonstrating perfect faith. Therefore, if we are to be as he is, it is plain that our faith must increase. Growing in faith as we progress in our discipleship is not an option: God expects it of us.

In a situation which they found particularly challenging, *the apostles said to the Lord, "Increase our faith!"* Jesus' response contains some of the most direct and forceful teaching of his ministry. One senses in it the same barely-contained frustration that surfaced in the healing scene which followed his transfiguration: *"O unbelieving and perverse generation,"* Jesus replied, *"how long shall I stay with you and put up with you?."* *(Luke 9:41)*

First *(Luke 17:6)*, he says, in effect: "You've got all the faith you need. Just use it!" Then *(v7-10)* he tells the story of a man and his servant. The servant has laboured all day in the fields and is tired, but before he can feed himself and rest, he must first prepare and serve his master's meal. Meaning what?

"Put God's service first and your own needs second. Keep your eyes on me and the work of the kingdom, and you'll find that you have faith and to spare." Put another way, Jesus is saying: "Man, its not faith you need more of, its obedience. You are mine now, you are under orders. Quit looking inwards at your failures and start moving mountains in obedience to my commands. Just do it!"

About half of Jesus' recorded statements on faith are to the lack of it. 'Little faith', 'lack of faith', 'unbelief', regularly disturbed him. As we review the things we can do to increase our faith, let us keep in our sights the truth that faith, like the love of God to which it is indissolubly joined, must be used in obedience to the Spirit's directions if it is not to waste away. You can study faith until you are blue in the face and a global expert on it, but if you want to please Jesus - just use it!

"Every area that we use our faith should bring glory to God."
(Andrew Wommack)[10]

Glory has come to me through them. (John 17:10)

Summary.

The burden of Jesus' teaching on faith is that each of us already has all the faith we need. Paul reflected this truth in speaking of *the measure of faith God has given you (Romans 12:3).* Like the Holy Spirit and the gifts of the Spirit, faith is resident within us. Jesus' prescription for victorious living is not 'more faith' but 'more obedience and less unbelief'. Our focus now shifts, therefore, to what we can do to counteract these negative factors.

The master key to faith.

The sole and entire reason for existence of the biblical concept of faith is to describe the manner of our interaction with the unseen and eternal God. It is the umbilical cord joining the developing believer, whose life is hid with Christ in God, to the Father. It is mysterious, supernatural and, above all, real.

So we fix our eyes not on what is seen, but on what is unseen. For what is seen is temporary, but what is unseen is eternal. (2 Corinthians 4:18)

"True faith is the recognition of who God is."
(Rick Joyner)[11]

If there are keys to growing in faith, then this is the master key: to be certain, if necessary to the point of dying for it, of the reality of the unseen and eternal God. More, it is to be utterly convinced that the unseen and the eternal is the greater reality, compared with the ever-present, insistent and intrusive world of time and space in which we are but aliens and strangers who have no permanent abode. If we are certain that our citizenship is in heaven; that all of our life in every aspect is to be determined in the light of eternity; if our heart is consumed by our intimate, personal relationship with God; then faith will not be a problem. Such is the 'perfect heart' which God desires and of which the scriptures speak repeatedly. These are the ones he strengthens, and speaks to as a man does to his friend.

For the eyes of the LORD range throughout the earth to strengthen those whose hearts are fully committed to him. (2 Chronicles 16:9)

The LORD would speak to Moses face to face, as a man speaks with his friend. (Exodus 33:11)

I no longer call you servants, because a servant does not know his master's business. Instead, I have called you friends, for everything that I learned from my Father I have made known to you." (John 15:15)

If you would have great faith, then give yourself wholly and unreservedly to God, allow his Spirit to overwhelm and consume you. To follow this path requires, inevitably, separation from the world, its blandishments and standards. Some compromise, surrounding themselves with as many of the comforts, riches and honours of this world as they deem to be consistent with their profession of faith in Christ - and then wonder why they have so little of it.

Faith is about our relationship with God. Set aside the super-confident 'name it and claim it' faith teaching which abounds today, and tremble before the Holy One, by whose great mercies we are not consumed.

"The clearer and more deliberate, the more conscious the decision is for the unseen, the more will faith in God be strengthened and rewarded. ... The great work faith has to do, and the best school for its growth and strength, is the choice of the unseen." (Andrew Murray)[12]

"Nothing hinders faith and the operation of the Spirit so much as the self-assertiveness of the human soul, the wisdom, strength, and self-sufficiency of the human mind. This must all be crucified, and here is where the fight comes in. .... We want the Holy Spirit, but the fact is that He is wanting possession of us."
(Frank Bartelman)[13]

Other keys to growing in faith.

Since faith involves knowledge, trust and action, it follows that attention to each of these aspects has a bearing on the development of faith. The 'master key' described above deals with the central element of trust.

Faith component	Key to growth
Knowledge	Time in the word.
Trust	Fellowship with God. (The master key)
Action	Obedience.

In Chapter 3 we noted several hindrances to faith which were deduced logically on the basis of the model of Figure 3.1. These hindrances fall naturally into two groups which correspond to the 'knowledge' and 'action' components. If all such hindrances were eliminated we would operate in great faith.

The key of the knowledge of God's word.

Faith comes in seed form. Like any physical seed it will grow into its intended mature form only if planted in good soil, watered and tended. Nothing stimulates this process like meditating on the word of God, the Bible, because all faith is based upon a word from God. If we are to live as Jesus did, speaking and doing only what the Father gives, it follows that knowing and hearing God's word is a key issue, and that's our responsibility. It is a matter of Christian witness that God is heard most clearly and consistently through scripture. Therefore, dwell in the word.

Let the word of Christ dwell in you richly as you teach and admonish one another with all wisdom, and as you sing psalms, hymns and spiritual songs with gratitude in your hearts to God. (Colossians 3:16)

Do not let this Book of the Law depart from your mouth; meditate on it day and night, so that you may be careful to do everything written in it. (Joshua 1:8)

Psalm 119 is the overflow of a life steeped in God's word. All but one of its 176 verses contains one of eight synonyms of God's will: 'law', 'word', statutes', 'testimony', 'judgements'   or   'ordinances',   'precepts',   'way', 'commandments'.

*I seek you with all my heart; do not let me stray from
your commands. (v10)
Your statutes are my delight; they are my counsellors. (v24)
Great peace have they who love your law, and nothing
can make them stumble. (v165)*

Dwelling in the word is also our best protection from spiritual deception. *Your word is a lamp to my feet and a light for my path (Psalm 119:105).* Jesus' condemnation of the Pharisees and Sadducees was often directed at their ignorance of the scriptures. He said to them things like: *Have you never read in the Scriptures ...? (Matthew 21:42); You are in error because you do not know the Scriptures or the power of God (Matthew 22:29).* Knowledge of scripture was never more vital than in these, the last days, because even the elect are in danger of being deceived (*Matthew 24:24*).

As you dwell in the word of God, your heart becomes softened towards it. Hardness of heart comes primarily from inadequate exposure to and belief in God's word, and unbelief is the product of a hardened heart. Jesus taught plainly that unbelief prevents God from working.

Jesus said to them, "Only in his hometown, among his relatives and in his own house is a prophet without honour." He could not do any miracles there, except lay his hands on a few sick people and heal them. And he was amazed at their lack of faith. (Mark 6:4-6)

Therefore, if you would move in great faith, dwell in the scriptures daily, even hourly, meditating upon them, like the writer of *Psalm 119*. As your mind is renewed by the word (*Romans 12:2*), so unbelief will melt away. God is always faithful to his word. Our part, our work, is to choose to discipline ourselves to dwell in the scriptures and thereby to learn his *logos*, and to be open to hear his *rhema* words to us.

Do not let this Book of the Law depart from your mouth; meditate on it day and night, so that you may be careful to do everything written in it. Then you will be prosperous and successful. (Joshua 1:8)

Oh, how I love your law! I meditate on it all day long. (Psalm 119:97)

Seven times a day I praise you for your righteous laws. (Psalm 119:164)

"Faith is primarily thinking ..... and the whole trouble with a man of little faith is that he does not think. He allows circumstances to bludgeon him. The way to avoid that, according to our Lord, is to think. Christian faith is essentially thinking. Look at the birds, says Jesus, think about them and draw your deductions. Look at the grass, look at the lilies of the field, consider them. The trouble with most people, however, is that they will not think. Instead of doing this they sit down and ask, what is going to happen to me? What can I do? That is the absence of thought; it is surrender, it is defeat. We are entitled to define 'little faith' as being a failure to think, of allowing life to master our thoughts instead of thinking clearly about it." (Martyn Lloyd-Jones)[14]

The key of obedience.

The Christian's life is to be one of continual obedience to the Father's initiatives. Like Jesus, we are not to live by bread alone, *but on every word that comes from the mouth of the Lord (Deuteronomy 8:3)*. That is, we are to learn to be in such a relationship of continuing dependency that, like Jesus, we shall only do what we see the Father do, and say what we hear from him.

Faith involves action in response to a word from God - which is obedience by another name. Disobedience is rebellion and inevitably leads to sin. Thus, Paul's statement that *everything that does not come from faith is sin (Romans 14:23)*. We see now why it is that *without faith it is impossible to please God (Hebrews 11:6)*. To be without faith is to be in unbelief, which is a state of wilful refusal to act on the known word of God.

Obedience is the fruit of love: faith, love and obedience go together, and characterise the spiritually healthy Christian. In contrast, unbelief, hatred and disobedience typify the dysfunctional Christian who does not please God, and whose will reigns where the Spirit of God should hold sway.

We have been chosen .... for obedience to Jesus Christ. (1 Peter 1:2)

Disobedience may result, also, from refusal to resolve doubts. Such procrastination may indicate that the things of God are low in our order of priorities. Fear of man, of what others may think, can result in disobedience. Knowledge of 'who I am in God' should deal with this.

However, when all these factors have been identified, it remains true that disobedience to the word of God indicates a heart issue, a malfunction of our personal relationship with Jesus. The crux of the matter is: shall it be his will or mine? He must be Lord of all, or he is not Lord at all. Come to him in repentance and humility of heart. Allow him to do whatever is needed in you.

Continuing in faith: perseverance.

If you do not stand firm in your faith, you will not stand at all." (Isaiah 7:9)

It is by faith you stand firm. (2 Corinthians 1:24)

We continually remember before our God and Father your work produced by faith, your labour prompted by love, and your endurance inspired by hope in our Lord Jesus Christ. (1 Thessalonians 1:3)

"True faith is not a single step but a long walk."
(David Pawson)[15]

The emotive term the *fight of faith* is used just once in the NT (*1 Timothy 6:12*), although there are many instances in which the same attitude is reflected in different words. The 'fight' comes in the context of persevering in our belief in God's word to us, even when it is at variance with circumstances. Will we live by the observable facts, or by the truth of God's word? The Bible tells us that it is *through faith and patience that we inherit the promises of God (Hebrews 6:12)*, and that *you need to persevere so that when you have done the will of God, you will receive what he has promised (Hebrews 10:36)*.

In persevering, the scriptures are to be our encouragement, thereby enabling us to maintain that godly hope which will see us through to the answers for which we are praying (*Romans 15:4*). Encouragement also is a gift of God (*Romans 15:5*).

"True faith is perseverance in the midst of the storm. True faith is the trait most demonstrated in the life of the apostle Paul, who not only fought the good fight but finished the race and kept his faith. Paul's faith, like that of Job, was not fixed on the temporary circumstances of life but on the Author and Finisher of faith, on Christ himself." (Hank Hanegraaff)[16]

"Learning to live by faith is learning to make the right choices, believing God no matter how you feel or what others say." (Colin Urquhart)

These qualities of perseverance, patience and endurance develop in us with increasing spiritual maturity, being part of 'the fruit of the Spirit'. In particular, it is the testing of our faith that generates perseverance. Thus, James and Paul encouraged the church:

Consider it pure joy, my brothers, whenever you face trials of many kinds, because you know that the testing of your faith develops perseverance. Perseverance must finish its work so that you may be mature and complete, not lacking anything. (James 1:2-4)

Not only so, but we also rejoice in our sufferings, because we know that suffering produces perseverance; perseverance,

*character; and character, hope. And hope does not disappoint
us, because God has poured out his love into our hearts by the
Holy Spirit, whom he has given us. (Romans 5:3-5)*

We know that faith and love operate together in that our
obedient faith action in response to God's revealed will is also
the sign of our love for him. It follows that if we are to persevere
in faith, we must also persevere in love. Thus, Paul, writing of
love notes that: *it always protects, always trusts, always hopes,
always perseveres. (1 Corinthians 13:7)* Added force is given to this
observation by appreciating that we are included in God's new
covenant of love in which he will always persevere.

1.
*Safe home, safe home in port!
Rent cordage, shattered deck
Torn sails, provision short
And only not a wreck.
But O the joy upon the shore
To tell the voyage perils o'er.*

2.
*The prize, the prize secure!
The athlete nearly fell
Bare all he could endure
And bare not always well.
But he may smile at troubles gone
Who sets the victor garland on.*

3.
*No more the foe can harm
No more of leaguered camp
And cry of night alarm
And need of ready lamp.
And yet how nearly has he failed
How nearly had that foe prevailed.*

4.
The exile is at home
O nights and days of tears
O longings not to roam
O sins and doubts and fears.
What matters now grief's darkest day?
The King has wiped those tears away.

Joseph the Hymnographer (9th century)
Free translation by John Mason Neale
(1818-66)[17]

CHAPTER 5.

Living by Faith

Preview. The theme in this Chapter is: living by faith. The principle of first discerning God's will, and then acting on it, is shown to underly every area in which faith is used. Application is made specifically, to (1) faith for meeting with God, and (2) faith for healing.

God, the focus of our faith.

The Christian life is one of faith from start to finish. The same faith principles apply in every area of Christian life, work and witness. The same faith thinking lies behind all prayer, all healing, and every issue of Christian discipleship and conduct.

Faith has three components: trust, knowledge and action. Our trust (faith, confidence) is in God himself. His nature and character are utterly trustworthy. He is totally faithful to his word of truth. The nature and character of God is the bedrock of our faith. Therefore Jesus said: *Have faith in God (Mark 11:22).* The use of faith in any and every situation resolves, therefore, into settling two questions:

Q1. What has God said? What is his will about this
issue now facing me?

Q2. What am I to do? What is my resulting faith action?

Of these, the first and crucial question is: 'Lord, what is
your will in this situation?' Our focus is to be on God, upon
what he is saying and doing.

Using faith always begins by focusing on one simple issue: 'Lord, what is your will in this situation?'

This may seem simple and obvious, but the Spirit insists
that it be emphasised here. In these end-times, God is forming a
new breed of believer, and a church that knows its power and
authority in God and is ready to dominate the powers of
darkness. This people will have their hearts focused on God as
never before. Therefore, he will be able to release faith for the
miraculous on an entirely new level. Why? Because biblical faith
is rooted in and focussed on God himself. If it is not, then faith
becomes a sterile formula.

Faith is not a formula.
Faith is not a formula. To focus only on the word as the
basis of faith leads to a faith which is more intellectual than
spiritual. Certainly faith must be based upon what God has
said, but it is also about our continuing lifestyle of fellowship
with God, through which the unseen becomes as real and
certain as material things.

Why does the Spirit insist that I make this point?
Because the focus of the church is too much man-centred. The
righteous will live by his faith (*Habakkuk 2:4*), not by his reading
of Christian books and articles, his tasting of sermons and
conferences, and his following after personalities and
ministries. **God will have his people depend upon himself
alone.**

Please understand that this is not an anti-intellectual stance. Praise God for anointed Christian authors, publishers, and ministries: their work is of prime value in discipling and inspiring the Church. But also hear this: God insists that each and every believer shall learn to turn first and foremost to him, his Spirit and his word. It's like a new reformation. This is in the very nature of the end-time Church now being revealed.

> *As for you, the anointing you received from him remains in you, and you do not need anyone to teach you. But as his anointing teaches you about all things and as that anointing is real, not counterfeit—just as it has taught you, remain in him. (1 John 2:27)*

The 16th century Reformation recovered this same truth, that *the righteous will live by his faith*, by his faith alone, and not by the authority and intermediary of the church which had by then distanced the individual believer from God. Today God is saying to his Church that the focus must shift back to himself: *the righteous will live by his faith.*

> "God is a supernatural, incomprehensible being; we must learn to know him in a way that is above reason and sense. That way is the adoration of faith, and the deep humility of obedience. Through these the Holy Spirit will work the work of God in us." (Andrew Murray)[1]

Faith is based on relationship with God.

We now see how that works in practice. In each area of application we shall seek to answer the above two faith questions. In doing so we shall see that there is a simplicity and unity of practice encompassing every area in which we use our faith, in prayer, healing, prophesy, evangelism, and much else besides. Nevertheless, let it be said again that faith does not work on the basis of a formula, but out of our intimate fellowship with God. In the course of that fellowship we feel his heart, and therefore hear his word of command. Our subsequent obedience then makes our faith complete and pleasing to God. The next section not only illustrates these truths, but also forms the context within which all other uses of faith are birthed.

Faith for meeting with God.

The great theme of the Bible is that God created us in love to know him, love, trust, and be satisfied by him. Adam and Eve enjoyed intimacy of fellowship with God in Eden. They lost it because of sin, and in consequence were ejected from the garden, and therefore also from intimacy with God. Nevertheless, God did not give up on them but began to reveal a way back, hinting that an innocent sacrifice would be the key issue by making clothes of animal skins to cover their nakedness.

Through prophets from Moses onwards, he told the nation of Israel that he was their husband and that they were to regard themselves as his wife, the exclusivity and intimacy of marriage implying a like relationship with himself. The relationship tottered and failed, leading to announcement, first of separation, finally of divorce. Still the Holy One pursued his desire for intimacy with his creation. A new covenant was announced, on which basis re-marriage would occur.

During the centuries, or millennia, from Adam and Eve onwards, it was possible to worship God only at a distance. But now, because of Christ, that is history. As Jesus died on the cross as the ultimate Passover sacrifice, in the Jerusalem temple the curtain which separated the Holy Place from the Holy of Holies was torn in two, indicating that the way into God's very presence is now open to all believers.

Through the gift of the Holy Spirit at Pentecost, all believers now enjoy an intimacy of fellowship with God which exceeds that enjoyed by Adam and Eve. This is possible because we have been cleansed by the blood of Christ. Therefore, the Holy

One may now dwell in us. We *literally participate in the divine nature (2 Peter 1:4)*, and even better is to come because this is but *a deposit guaranteeing our inheritance (Ephesians 1:14)*. Meanwhile, we are part of the church, the body of Christ, who is being prepared as the Bride of Christ, thereby to usher in the final consummation of God's purpose, the New Jerusalem.

The sustained, passionate heart behind this cosmic love-affair of God with his errant creation is awesome, breathtaking, and utterly humbling. The Almighty longs for my love, and gave Jesus to enable me to come close to him!

God told Moses that in the Holy of Holies he would meet with him one-to-one. It is still true. He meets with the individual believer one-to-one. How? By faith!

> *In him [Jesus] and through faith in him we may approach God with freedom and confidence. (Ephesians 3:12)*

> *Therefore, brothers, since we have confidence to enter the Most Holy Place by the blood of Jesus, by a new and living way opened for us through the curtain, that is, his body, and since we have a great priest over the house of God, let us draw near to God with a sincere heart in full assurance of faith, having our hearts sprinkled to cleanse us from a guilty conscience and having our bodies washed with pure water. (Hebrews 10:19-22)*

The first calling on every believer's life is ministry to God, because he has made us *a royal priesthood (1 Peter 2:9)*. For this we have been created, chosen and called. Scripture is littered with expressions of the heart-cry of God, repeated through one prophet after another, to *seek his face (Psalm 27)*. *Call to me and I will answer you (Jeremiah 33:3); knock and the door will be opened to you (Matthew 7:7)*.

Thus, the answer to the *first of our two faith questions* is established beyond doubt. God's will is that everyone in his kingdom seek his face and enter his presence. This we call 'meeting with God'. This should be our intent and expectation every time we pray, and whenever we worship: to meet with God in one-to-one intimacy, to minister to him, to know the impact of his Spirit on our spirit. Jesus gave his life to open this way for us.

Now for the *second question:* What is my faith action in this instance? Answer: to believe, and to respond to God's will and word by meeting with him. In doing this it's helpful to have a platform of scripture: any of those in the preceding paragraphs will do, as will many others. For example:

> *After this I looked, and there before me was a door standing open in heaven. And the voice I had first heard speaking to me like a trumpet said, "Come up here, and I will show you what must take place after this." At once I was in the Spirit, and there before me was a throne in heaven with someone sitting on it. (Revelation 4:1-2)*

Meeting with God.

Beloved, please join me now in reaching out to God. Use your imagination, see yourself entering through that open door, see the glory streaming through it, enveloping you as you approach the Father's throne. Open your heart to him, be real. He knows everything about you anyway, and every thought in your head, so its no big deal to be totally honest with him. Step out confidently knowing for certain that he will respond to you. Make this decision: "I give up all reservations about letting my Lord touch my heart. I will fall into his arms of love, knowing that he will keep me in perfect safety. No harm can come to me because he loves me perfectly and will always protect me". You know, scripture says: *God has not given us a spirit of fear, but of power and of love and of a sound mind (2 Timothy 1:7 NKJV).* The Greek original actually means: *a safe mind.*

So start speaking to him now. Tell him that you love him. Tell him the things that are on your heart. He will respond. But keep your focus on him, not on your own concerns, and bear in mind the wise advice of King Solomon:

God is in heaven and you are on earth, so let your words be few.
(Ecclesiastes 5:2)

Listen more than you speak, but begin now by speaking: "Lord, I love you, I want to know you better. Holy One, I open my heart to you, I rejoice because I'm no longer my own but yours, and you are directing my life." Continue to pour out your heart in your own words, but leave plenty of time, plenty of time, for him to respond. Let the Holy Spirit take charge of your praying: don't insist on setting the agenda but, equally, don't sink into a passive state. Love him, just love him!

As the Holy Spirit impacts your spirit you will know that you are meeting with God. You will feel clean and know that you are forgiven, totally accepted in his presence. Sometimes its like standing under a waterfall of love.

"The Spirit of prayer comes upon a man and drives him into the depths of the heart, as if he were taken by the hand and forcibly led from one room to another. The soul is here taken captive by an invading force, and is kept willingly within, as long as this overwhelming power of prayer still holds sway over it." (Theophan the Recluse, a Russian Orthodox monk)[2]

Avoiding mysticism.

What is there to distinguish such worship from mysticism? The mystic seeks truth through feelings, visions, imagination and other subjective means. It was a tendency of the charismatic movement. In our worship, and in seeking

God's face, we are on safe ground if we hold to the following principles.

1. Minister to God. The aim of our worship is to glorify God and to minister to him by pouring out our hearts to him in praise and adoration. The aim is not to seek 'warm fuzzy' feelings for our souls. Of course, he responds to such worship and, yes, feelings and emotions are involved, as in any loving relationship, but if our focus is kept on him, we shall not drift into self-centred mysticism. Rather, we shall be carried along by the Holy Spirit (*2 Peter 1:21*), and taken from stream to stream (*Psalm 46:4*) of the supernatural river of God (*Ezekiel 47*), which is for every saint to enjoy and to drink from (*John 7:37*).

2. Do all according to scripture. In our worship it is most important that we sing hymns and songs which glorify God. So many modern songs are feelings-centred, or simply not scriptural: they drag worship down into soulish realms. Let everything we sing be either in the words of scripture, or based directly upon scripture.

Singing, clapping, raising hands, shouting, and dancing are all part of biblical worship, but all should be done in response to the Spirit's leading.

Faith and healing.

God's nature is always to meet his people's need. The many OT Jehovaistic names of God are but one expression of this truth. Specifically, Jehovah-Rapha: *I am the Lord who heals you (Exodus 15:26)*. More particularly, Isaiah prophesied ca.750 BC of the coming Messiah that he would be the source of healing in the widest sense, in respect of physical wounds, sicknesses, relationships and even sorrows.

> *Surely he took up our infirmities and carried our sorrows, yet we considered him stricken by God, smitten by him, and afflicted. But he was pierced for our transgressions, he was*

*crushed for our iniquities; the punishment that brought us
peace was upon him, and by his wounds we are healed.*
(Isaiah 53:4-5)
He heals the broken-hearted, and binds up their wounds.
(Psalm 147:3)

Peter quoted from Isaiah: *By his wounds you have been
healed (1 Peter 2:24).* Note the tense of the verb: *you **have been
healed**.* Its a done deal! Christ paid the price at Calvary, defeated
Satan, and won for us both life and comprehensive healing. In
his earthly ministry, teaching and healing went hand in hand,
the healings (and other signs and wonders) validating the
spoken word. That same ministry is bequeathed to the church.

*I tell you the truth, anyone who has faith in me will do what I
have been doing. He will do even greater things than these,
because I am going to the Father. (John 14:12)*

*And these signs will accompany those who believe: In my name
they will drive out demons; ..... they will place their hands on
sick people, and they will get well." (Mark 16:17-18)*

Evangelism and healing should go together: the
connection is very close. The Greek word *sozo* is usually
translated as 'save', but also as 'heal' (*Mark 5:23*), and is used to
refer to the healing brought by deliverance from demonic
possession (*Luke 8:36*).

God's desire is that all men shall be saved (*1 Timothy
2:4*), and few Christians doubt that. Strange, therefore, that so
many do not accept that God's will is also to heal and deliver his
people. But it is! Let us be confident, not only that it is God's will
to heal, but also that he has already provided it at Calvary.

This answers the *first* of our two faith questions. The
second question (What is my faith action?) is illuminated by
asking how Jesus handled the healing ministry.

Healing in Jesus' ministry.

Jesus always met that those who came for healing at the level of their faith. He didn't seem to mind too much about the form of its expression, but he usually wanted to see some evidence of it. Two people, both foreigners, amazed him by showing 'great faith': a Roman Centurion (*Matthew 8:5-13*) and a Canaanite woman (*Matthew 15:21-28*). In each case the sick person, although not actually present, was healed by an authoritative word from him.

A little further down the faith scale were those who required physical contact with Jesus to receive their healing: a leper (*Matthew 8:1-3*); two blind men at Jericho (*Matthew 20:29-34*); a woman with a haemorrhage, *If I only touch his cloak, I will be healed (Matthew 9:20-22)*.

Sometimes he would seek to build faith before commanding the healing: *"Do you believe that I am able to do this?" "Yes, Lord" they replied (Matthew 9:28).* In other cases, some faith action was required of, or on behalf of, the sick person. *'Stretch out your hand '(Matthew 12:10-13);"Go," he told him, "wash in the Pool of Siloam". So the man went and washed, and came home seeing. (John 9:7);* Jesus replied, *"You may go. Your son will live." The man took Jesus at his word and departed (John 4:50).*

Thus, Jesus established the principle by which he worked: *"According to your faith will it be done to you" (Matthew 9:29).* This applies generally, not just in the area of healing.

Three faith inputs.

In general, three faith inputs are active in a healing situation: that of the sick person, and of the one ministering; and the faith of others who may be present - call it 'third-party faith'.

Any kind of ministry is hampered by an atmosphere of unbelief. Thus, In his home town Jesus *could not do any miracles there, except lay his hands on a few sick people and heal them. And he was amazed at their lack of faith (Mark 6:5-6).* For this reason Jesus sometimes took the sick person aside *(Mark 7:33),* surrounding them with the faith-shield of his disciples, before healing them. He first removed the mourners from Jairus' house before raising his daughter *(Mark 5:22-43);* and he advised a man whom he had healed of blindness not to return to his village (with its atmosphere of unbelief) if he wished to retain his healing *(Mark 8:22-26).* Third-party faith/unbelief is a significant factor in the healing ministry. In some churches its almost a spectator sport.

Healing non-believers.

In his great mercy, God will sometimes heal people who have no faith in Jesus for anything. A Pastor met an elderly man seriously disabled with arthritis. After a brief explanation about healing, the Pastor enquired if he should heal the man. "Go on then, if you want to", was the ungracious reply. He was healed progressively over the next few days, but still didn't want to know Jesus!

In such a case, the faith input is that of the one ministering, but he should also have the witness within that it is God's chosen moment to heal that person. Even Jesus didn't go about offering healing indiscriminately.

Healing believers.

By definition, the people Jesus healed were not Christians, but they were believers in his power to heal. Often the healing was the event which opened their inward eyes to see him as Son of God, and to become his followers. Today, it is through the healing that Jesus brings in evangelistic crusades that great numbers are entering the kingdom.

I love bringing healing to Muslims: like Christians they believe that Jesus is a prophet and that he heals. No problem, we have that in common. Lay hands on the sick person, speak the word of faith, and Jesus will do the healing. The sick Muslim will also be touched by God's love and may therefore be opened to a revelation of Jesus' divinity. Healing and the gospel are two sides of the same coin: they should always go together.

Our faith action in ministering healing.

Jesus did his part at Calvary. Therefore, we do not need to pray for healing: we simply believe and receive, just as we did to obtain salvation - there's no difference! You can receive your healing directly from God.

"Faith is our positive response to what God has already done." (Andrew Wommack)[3]

He said to her, "Daughter, your faith has healed you." (Mark 5:34)

In **ministering healing to others**, we do not need to pray, or to shout in tongues, or make a scene. Just do what Jesus did: respond to the faith level of the person who needs healing, and speak the word of command in faith. Remember, you have **authority** to heal and deliver. Its that easy so that God will get the glory. If we hype it up and make a great show of delivering healing, guess who gets some of the glory?

You see, God heals by his word. *He sent forth his word and healed them (Psalm 107:20).* As you speak in faith and with authority- "Jesus heals you!" - the healing comes. The word spoken in faith is powerful because *we also believe and therefore speak (2 Corinthians 4:13).* Commonly, you will also lay hands on the person as you command the healing.

The Spirit will show you also if it is necessary to prepare the way for the healing. Don't just lay on hands blindly without first discerning God's strategy. He may want to do something else first. Thus, common hindrances to receiving healing are unforgiveness and bitterness. If the response is: "I can't forgive", ask : "Are you willing to let God make you willing to forgive?"

On occasion it is necessary to bind the work of Satan in the person, before speaking the word of faith for healing. Smith Wigglesworth[4] always cursed a cancer before commanding it to go.

Sometimes, the situation may not be what it seems. In a Ukrainian hospital a lady came seeking healing for pains in her heart, but the Lord said: "Ask her about her family". One son had recently hanged himself, another was in a distant prison and her husband had gone there to try to help him out, two daughters were on drugs and into crime. No wonder she had pains in her heart! The real issue was to pray into her family situation.

"The real life of faith, of being a Christian, of receiving forgiveness or healing, is in knowing him."
(David Hathaway)

CHAPTER 6.

Faith and Prayer

Preview. The faith principles involved in prayer are outlined and applied to the two primary areas of: (1) prayer for ourselves; (2) prayer for others. The OT and the NT understandings of intercession are distinguished. The issue of the time delay associated with prayer answers is discussed.

Faith and prayer.

Prayer is the whole of our interaction with God, the expression of our intimate, personal relationship with him. It is not limited to those times when we get apart 'to pray', or when we are in prayer meetings. However, we do need to understand how to pray for our needs and those of others, so that we may be efficient and effective in our praying.

If the axe is dull and its edge unsharpened, more strength is needed but skill will bring success. (Ecclesiastes 10:10)

"Faith is the essential quality in the heart of any man who desires to communicate with God. He must believe and stretch out the hands of faith for that which he cannot see or prove. Prayer is actually faith claiming and taking hold of its natural, immeasurable inheritance. ... Moreover, when faith ceases to pray, it ceases to live." (E.M. Bounds)1

When we pray we are not, as it were, grasping the horns of the altar and shaking it until God comes out. Prayer works by faith, and faith works on the basis of an expression of God's will. Therefore no prayer ever causes God to change his mind or to do something he has not already ordained. There are many kinds of prayer and it would be impossible for us to cover them all in a summary account like this. What we shall do is to address the two key faith questions and deduce their logical consequences in respect of prayer.

"Faith does not cause God to move. It takes what God has already done in the spiritual realm and brings it into the physical realm." (Andrew Wommack)

What has God said?

As we come to pray, the agenda needs to be set by the Holy Spirit, and for every issue the question to be settled is : 'What is God's will?' The word of God upon which faith for prayer depends is commonly in the form of one or more of the great prayer promises.

*Jesus replied, "I tell you the truth, **if you have faith and do not doubt**, not only can you do what was done to the fig tree, but also you can say to this mountain, 'Go, throw yourself into* *the sea,' and it will be done. **If you believe, you will receive whatever you ask for in prayer.**" (Matthew 21:21-22)*

*I tell you the truth, anyone who has faith in me will do what I have been doing. He will do even greater things than these, because I am going to the Father. And **I will do whatever you ask in my name**, so that the Son may bring glory to the Father. You may ask me for anything in my name, and I will do it. (John 14:12-14)*

*If you remain in me and my words remain in you, **ask whatever you wish, and it will be given you.** (John 15:7)*

These are the very words of Jesus. The inescapable conclusion is that God promises to answer the prayers offered in faith: he can do no other. *If you believe, you will receive whatever you ask for in prayer.*

This is the confidence we have in approaching God: that if we ask anything according to his will, he hears us. And if we know that he hears us—whatever we ask—we know that we have what we asked of him. (1 John 5:14-15)

My God will meet all your needs according to his glorious riches in Christ Jesus. (Philippians 4:19)

BUT ....

All scriptural promises are conditional.

Answered prayer brings glory to God, so it is important for us to know how to get answers consistently. The conditions associated with the above promises are: (1) have faith in God, and do not doubt; (2) ask in Jesus' name; (3) remain in Jesus, ensuring that his words are active in our hearts; (4) ask according to his will. These conditions are summed up in the understanding that *I have been crucified with Christ and I no longer live, but Christ lives in me (Galatians 2:20)*. Its his life lived in me, not my life lived in 'the God-kind of faith'.

These are very substantial 'if's', and they go a long way to accounting for many so-called unanswered prayers. Other common reasons for unanswered prayer are: (5) not living in forgiveness; (6) expecting a particular answer and being unwilling to accept a different one from God; (7) lawlessness (*Proverbs 28:9*); (8) and wrong motives (*James 4:3*) - you can pray the perfect will of God in your situation and still see no result unless your heart motives are pure.

Note also to whom these great prayer promises were given: the Apostles, and others close to Jesus. Do they apply to us also? Yes, but only insofar as we meet the conditions. The Apostles had thrown in their lot with Jesus, totally. They were not just followers, they were submitted to his lordship.

In the name of Jesus.
Abiding (remaining, dwelling) in him and being saturated with his words means that we shall view every situation from his perspective rather than our own. The Spirit of Jesus lives within us, and the Spirit *knows the thoughts of God (1 Corinthians 2:11)*. To the extent that we are listening to and are obedient to the Spirit, we will know what he is thinking, *we shall have the mind of Christ (1 Corinthians 2:16)*, and thus we shall ask the Father for the things Jesus would have us ask for in our circumstances. What we then ask is in keeping with the character of Jesus. In scripture a name is a reflection of that person's character, so by praying in character with Jesus we are praying in his name.

However, its more than that. In praying in Jesus' name we also pray with his authority. Its not unlike walking into a bank with a blank cheque signed by their most important customer. The Father promises to answer us as he would Jesus.

This, then, is the true meaning of *ask in my name*. Its not just a phrase we tack onto the ends of our prayers because we're supposed to: 'In Jesus' name, Amen'! Its not a formula; its about praying out of the heart of Jesus, and with his authority. All true prayer starts in heaven.

> *Whatever you do, whether in word or deed, do it all in the name of the Lord Jesus, giving thanks to God the Father through him. (Colossians 3:17)*

Prayer and relationships.

Our attitudes to others also affect our prayers. Thus, Jesus told his disciples, that *when you stand praying, if you hold anything against anyone, forgive him, so that your Father in heaven may forgive you your sins (Mark 11:25; see also Matthew 6:14-15).* Not loving others ensures that we do not have the light of God's revelation in our lives, and therefore that we cannot pray with understanding (*1John 2:9-11*).

Peter wrote: *Husbands, in the same way be considerate as you live with your wives, and treat them with respect as the weaker partner and as heirs with you of the gracious gift of life, so that nothing will hinder your prayers (1 Peter 3:7).* In family, church, at work, in every arena of life we are guaranteed to face relationship problems. But as we humble ourselves before God, allowing him to deal with those things in us which generate ungodly reactions towards others (i.e. strongholds), we shall see more consistent answers to our prayers.

Satan is also active in disturbing relationships. There is a spirit of offence (Greek: *skandalon*) which he uses against Christians. "Jesus' mission was to live amongst lost, blind, ignorant, stupid people - and he did it" (Mary Alice Isleib). *God was reconciling the world to himself in Christ, not counting men's sins against them. And he has committed to us the message of reconciliation (2 Corinthians 5:19).* As I seek God for understanding of the ways of others, he will use me to pray for them and to seek reconciliation, even with those who have been an offence to me.

Praying the will of God.

It cannot be stated too firmly that scriptural faith depends upon a word *from* God, not upon what I choose to say to him. I am to pray in faith on the basis of *his* will, because all true prayer starts in heaven. This is the direct opposite of the 'name it and claim it' school of teaching. Therefore, take time to find the will of God in your situation. His will and his heart are the same.

However, with the best intentions in the world, I am not always clear what God's will for me is, especially if my emotions are involved. What I do know is that his thoughts and ways are higher than mine (*Isaiah 55:8-9*), and that from my limited perspective I cannot see the wider implications of my situation, or indeed be sure how he plans to work in it. How am I to pray?

"Lord, from where I'm at now, this is what I'd like, this is what my heart is crying out for, and it seems to me to line up with your will. Nevertheless, Father, I submit to your will, and I choose to obey whatever is your word to me, no matter how much my flesh may scream 'no'."

What I am *not* to pray is: "Lord, this is what I want. I'm asking in faith, and I thank you that I have received it." Such a prayer fails to meet scriptural conditions. (1) It's not praying in Jesus' name, because he wouldn't pray anything other than the Father's will. (2) To the extent that we are acting in independence, we are not abiding in Jesus.

Going a little farther, he fell to the ground and prayed that if possible the hour might pass from him. "Abba, Father," he said, "everything is possible for you. Take this cup from me. Yet not what I will, but what you will" (Mark 14:35-36).

Now listen, you who say, "Today or tomorrow we will go to this or that city, spend a year there, carry on business and make money." Why, you do not even know what will happen tomorrow. What is your life? You are a mist that appears for a little while and then vanishes. Instead, you ought to say, "If it is the Lord's will, we will live and do this or that" (James 4:13-15).

"If you have a mustard seed of faith and its God's will, you can move a mountain. If you have a mountain of faith and its not God's will, you won't move a mustard seed." (J. John)[2]

The problem of the time delay.

If we pray in line with scripture, we are praying in his will and that prayer shall be answered. *Whatever you ask for in prayer, believe that you have received it, and it will be yours (Mark 11:24).* This answers the second faith question: "What am I to do?" Answer: Only believe! The problem so often is that there is a time delay between uttering the prayer and seeing the manifestation, Figures 6.1 & 6.2. Abraham had to wait 25 years for his promised son; Habakkuk was told to wait an unspecified time for the answer to his question; and Jesus taught of the need to persevere in prayer until the desired end is received (*Luke 18:1-8*).

Let's be clear about one thing: God hears and answers our prayers instantly. When the heavens are as brass and it seems that our prayer hasn't been answered, let us at least stand on this: he has heard me.

How gracious he will be when you cry for help!
As soon as he hears, he will answer you. (Isaiah 30:19)

Then Jesus looked up and said, Father, I thank you that you have heard me. (John 11:41)

Since the first day that you set your mind to gain

understanding and to humble yourself before God, your words were heard. (Daniel 10:12)

Your prayers and gifts to the poor have come up as a remembrance before God. (Acts 10:4)

Understand that when we pray in line with his will God hears and answers immediately. It may not seem to be so, but we are to receive the answers to our prayers by faith, waiting meanwhile in hope (i.e. confident, positive expectation) for the manifestation. Some prayers, by their very nature, are answered immediately as, for example, in crisis situations. With other prayers there may be a delay of days or years. Indeed, some saints will die without seeing the manifestation of their prayers (*cf. Hebrews 11:13, 39*), especially if those prayers are for long-term issues such as the revival of a nation. Those prayers are not wasted: they rise up before God's throne as a precious incense (*Revelation 8:3-4*), and they achieve their end because they are prayers 'in the Spirit' and therefore in eternity and not bounded by the limitations of time. Curious, then that even in, and indeed particularly in, the most traditional churches, congregations are happy to pray repeatedly a prayer which almost certainly will not be answered in all finality in their lifetimes.

Your kingdom come, your will be done, on earth as it is in heaven. (Matthew 6:10)

That prayer, uttered daily by millions of believers world-wide, is in the course of being answered. When Christ returns, finally it will be true that:

The kingdom of the world has become the kingdom of our Lord and of his Christ, and he will reign for ever and ever. (Revelation 11:15)

At that point in time God will have achieved his aim of restoring

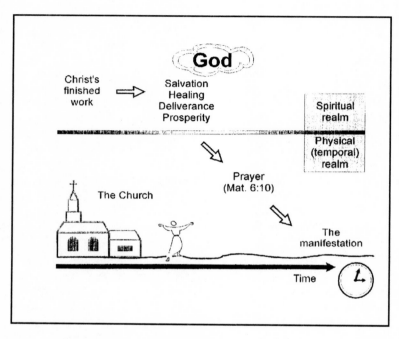

Figure 6.1
The purpose of prayer : to see Gods will done on earth.

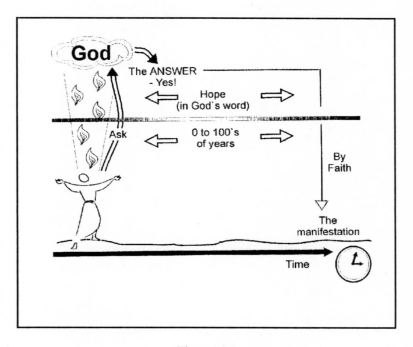

Figure 6.2
The time delay between praying and recieving
may be short or long.

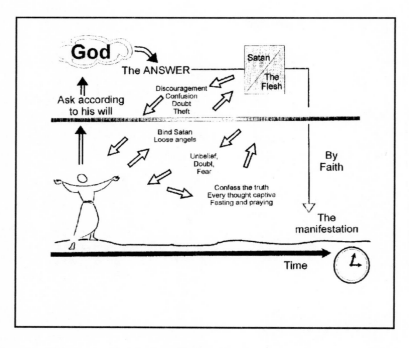

Figure 6.3
Dealing with the opression of (1) Satan, (2) the flesh life.

Eden-like life to earth. And that perfectly illustrates the entire purpose of prayer: it is to see God's will manifested on earth, as it is in heaven. Now, if only we can raise our sights from our personal and parochial concerns, and see ourselves as an integral and indispensable part of God's purpose for planet earth, we shall have far greater confidence that God hears and answers prayer, because in answering our prayers uttered in faith (even those for our personal needs and concerns), he will be bringing his kingdom in.

See yourself, therefore, not as an unimportant individual doing your inconsistent best to cope with the pressures of life, but as a child of God standing in kingdom authority before his throne of grace, asking for and receiving whatever you need that's in line with his will. His answer to your prayer is part and parcel of bringing in his kingdom on earth as it is in heaven. Does that put a different perspective on prayer? Hallelujah!

The purpose of prayer is to see God's will manifested on earth, as it is in heaven.

"We do de prayin', he do de doin'." (Alix Capon)

More about the time delay.
There are broadly three reasons for a time delay before we receive the manifestation of our prayer, Figure 6.3.

(1) God's timing. Jesus came to earth *when the time had fully come (Galatians 4:4).* The periods of the historical ascendancy of nations are of God's determining *(Acts 17:26). There is a time for everything, and a season for every activity under heaven (Ecclesiastes 3:1),* and God who is sovereign determines those times: we cannot alter them.

(2) Satan's opposition. Satan opposes everything that will bring glory to God. Therefore, it is part of prayer to use our authority to resist Satan, and to loose angels against him through worship and exaltation of Jesus. This is an aspect of spiritual warfare, and the key issue in that is having God's wisdom in dealing with the situation. Ask and you will receive that wisdom *(James 1:5)*.

(3) The flesh. If we lack understanding of how prayer works, and if we do not persevere in it, we may conclude that prayer doesn't work, at least for us. We may be unwilling to give the time and effort needed to pray effectually, or to crucify our own fleshly desires.

You do not have because you do not ask God. When you ask, you do not receive, because you ask with wrong motives. (James 4:2-3)

So do not throw away your confidence: it will be richly rewarded. You need to persevere so that when you have done the will of God, you will receive what he has promised. (Hebrews 10:35-36)

This understanding of reasons for the delay so often experienced between uttering a prayer and seeing the answer enables us to pray more confidently towards a breakthrough in each instance. Sometimes the wait is used by God to bring us into that place of faith in which we are able to receive his answer. I believe that's what was happening in Habakkuk. Having been assured that the answer to his prayer would come at the appointed time *(Habakkuk 2:2-4)* , he must have continued to think through the issues raised by the problem of innocent suffering with which he had challenged God. He failed to reach a conclusion but in the process discovered that trust in God's faithfulness was his bottom line. For him this crystallised in the revelation: *The righteous will live by his faith.* Now God could pour in the things he needed to know.

The prayer of a righteous man is powerful and effective. (James 5:16)

Praying in the Spirit.

This is the only kind of praying known to the NT. All true prayer is supernatural and therefore effective in the spiritual realm, and the spiritual realm controls the natural or temporal realm in which we live. Therefore:

Pray in the Spirit on all occasions with all kinds of prayers and requests. (Ephesians 6:18)

Prayer in the Spirit has three aspects. (1) Praying in your own mother tongue, and therefore with full understanding, based upon God's revealed will for that situation. (2) Praying in tongues. (3) Praying with tears, groans and such other manifestations as the Spirit may direct.

God's will, therefore, is that we pray in the Spirit. That deals with the first faith question. Now, "What am I to do?" Answer: start speaking.

Open wide your mouth and I will fill it. (Psalm 81:10)

Too simple?! As you come to pray, submit yourself and your agenda to God. Allow the Holy Spirit to take you into God's presence. Worship him, give thanks and praise. Ask his direction and wisdom. You may find that his order of priorities differs from yours, and new perspectives are liable to open up, as they did for the psalmist (*Psalm 73:16-17*). Pray in tongues and in your own language alternately so that you know what is going on. Let the prayer rise out of your inmost being: then you are praying from the Holy of Holies.

Situations often arise in which we really don't know what we should pray. Then we can pray in tongues.

The Spirit helps us in our weakness. We do not know what we ought to pray for, but the Spirit himself intercedes for us with groans that words cannot express. And he who searches our hearts knows the mind of the Spirit, because the Spirit intercedes for the saints in accordance with God's will. (Romans 8:26-27)

As we pray in tongues the Spirit will often given some understanding of what we are praying. Specifically, also, he will show us when to stop because the end has been achieved and the prayer answered, even 'though we may have to wait to see the result.

Applications.

Having established the general framework of faith by which prayer works we are in a position to look briefly at the two major areas of application: (1) praying for our own needs, and (2) for those of others.

The prayer of faith.

Every prayer should be a prayer of faith but, curiously, the label 'the prayer of faith' is often applied only to prayer for personal needs and those of our families. It is a definite prayer for a definite purpose, prayed with the understanding, not in tongues. Whatever the need, there is a scriptural promise which applies to it - this is what God has said about your situation.

Second question (see p 73): "What am I to do?" Answer: believe the promise and by faith receive the answer, reckoning it to be yours even before you see it. That's why it's called 'the prayer of faith'.

Whatever you ask for in prayer, believe that you have received it, and it will be yours. (Mark 11:24)

Do not be anxious about anything, but in everything, by prayer and petition, with thanksgiving, present your requests to God. And the peace of God, which transcends all understanding, will guard your hearts and your minds in Christ Jesus. (Philippians 4:6-7)

Insofar as we can see, in the natural, physical realm nothing has changed yet, but in the spiritual, supernatural realm it has and the result will be apparent in due time. There's no need to repeat the prayer until you see the answer. Ask once, then continue to stand in thankfulness and rejoicing, refusing to accept anything other than the desired answer. Perseverance is required in this second phase of the prayer for two reasons. (1) To deal with discouragement and anything else the devil may throw into the situation; (2) to allow God to deal with anything in us which may be delaying the result, and/or to show us some faith action which is required.

A powerful variant of this way of praying is the prayer of agreement in which two or more people agree together before God to stand in faith for a specific request (*Matthew 18:19*).

Intercession.
I urge, then, first of all, that requests, prayers, intercession and thanksgiving be made for everyone ... (1 Timothy 2:1)

The principle of intercession is identification: its about standing in the place of others, praying for their needs and on their behalf so that God's will for them shall be fulfilled and his kingdom extended. In contrast to the one-shot 'prayer of faith', intercession means praying repeatedly until the will of God is released into that situation. An understanding of factors that delay manifestation of the answer is especially relevant here.

The problem of will.
The problem about praying for others, as opposed to yourself, is that their will is also involved. God will not change a person's will, the devil cannot, and neither can we. I can align my own will with God's word, pray the prayer of faith, and continue in hope and thanksgiving until the answer comes.

With intercession it's different. I can pray the will and the word of God over that situation, (e.g. for salvation of a relative), I can ask God to send people across their path to witness to them, and I can bind the work of Satan in their life, but I can never change their will for them. Therefore, intercession is a process which may need to continue on any one topic for a very long time.

> "In intercession, we keep praying and praying until we sense the victory, until the breakthrough comes, or until the Holy Spirit discharges us from the case."
> (Mary Alice Isleib)[3]

The difference between OT and NT intercession.

This is a most important and much misunderstood issue. Abraham pleaded with God over the impending destruction of Sodom (*Genesis 18:16-33*), and Moses deflected God's anger at the rebellious rabble he was leading in Sinai (*Numbers 14*). Jesus did the same, only with this difference: that once, finally and for all eternity he paid the full price for the sins of the whole world, thereby permanently averting God's anger from those who believe in him (*John 4:36; Romans 2:5*). Hence, the NT intercessor is not struggling with God to get him to do something, or standing in the gap to stay his wrath. NT intercession is a matter of enforcing the victory Jesus won on the cross. Therefore, its a matter of:

1. Praying God's will in each situation.

2. Fighting off the opposition, standing in your delegated kingdom authority.

The devil prowls around like a roaring lion looking for someone to devour (1 Peter 5:8), trying to give the impression of authority, but actually he's a serpent doing an impression of a lion, and he has been comprehensively defeated at Calvary. Therefore, *resist him, standing firm in the faith (v9),* and he must flee. Wherever we find evidence of his activity (oppression, possession, depression, confusion, or any kind of trouble) we are to apply Christ's victory, use our delegated authority, and resist him. This is part of the work of intercession. It is essential to clear the ground, *to prepare the way for the Lord, (and) make straight in the wilderness a highway for our God (Isaiah 40:3).* Remember, in dealing with the devil its a truth encounter (God's truth versus the devil's lies), not a power contest.

The positive aspect of intercession is to pray the will of God into the situation you are facing. One excellent way of doing this is to *pray scripture.* Pray the biblical promises, claiming them for those you are praying for. By such means:

"we can cause the Word of God to run swiftly, obstacles to be removed, souls to be saved in multitudes, the preaching of the gospel to be followed by signs and wonders, as we pray in faith". (Francis Wale Oke)[4]

Glory to God!

See the Conqueror mounts in triumph
See the King in royal state
Riding on the clouds his chariot
To his heavenly palace gate.
Hark! the choirs of angel voices
Joyful hallelujahs sing
And the portals high are lifted
To receive their heavenly King.

Who is this that comes in glory
With the trump of jubilee?
Lord of battles, God of armies
He has gained the victory
He who on the cross did suffer
He who from the grave arose
He has vanquished sin and Satan
He by death has spoiled his foes.

He has raised our human nature
In the clouds to God's right hand
There we sit in heavenly places
There with him in glory stand
Jesus reigns, adored by angels
Man with God is on the throne
Mighty Lord, in thine ascension
We by faith behold our own.

Glory be to God the Father
Glory be to God the Son
Dying, risen, ascended for us
Who the heavenly realm has won.
Glory to the Holy Spirit
To One God in persons three
Glory both in earth and heaven
Glory, endless glory be!

Bishop Christopher Wordsworth (1807-85)[5]

REFERENCES

Chapter 1

1.1 *The Holiest of All* Andrew Murray, Whitaker House, Springdale, Pa, USA 1996 [First published: London, England 1895] p421.

1.2 *Pocket Guide to Christian Beliefs* I. Howard Marshall, IVP, Leicester, England 1963.

1.3 *Insights into Faith* Andrew Wommack, Andrew Wommack Ministries Inc., Colorado Springs, Co, USA 1980, p34.

1.4 Ref. 1.1, p422.

1.5 *Reckless Faith* John F. MacArthur, Crossway Books, Wheaton, Ill, USA 1994, p138.

1.6 *Faith, What a Deal!* Dave Duell, Faith Ministries Press, Greely, Co, USA 1992, p128.

1.7 *A Glimpse of Glory* Kathryn Kuhlman, Bridge Publ. Inc., New Jersey, USA 1983, p45.

Chapter 2

2.1 *Expository Dictionary of Bible Words* W.E. Vine, Marshall Morgan & Scott, Basingstoke, Hants., England, 1981, p2-71.

2.2 *The Knowledge of the Holy* A.W. Tozer, STL Books, Bromley, Kent, England, 1976.

2.3 *Christ the Healer* F.F. Bosworth, Fleming H. Revell, Grand Rapids, Michigan, USA, 1973, p5.

2.4 Ref. 1.5, p xiii.

2.5 *Every Day with Jesus* Selwyn Hughes, CWR, Farnham, Surrey, England, 28 July 1994

2.6 Ref: 2.5, 18 August 1994

2.7 *Biography of James Hudson Taylor* Dr & Mrs Howard Taylor, Hodder & Stoughton, London, England, 1973, p348.

2.8 *Systematic Theology,* Wayne Grudem, IVP, Leicester, England, 1994, p730.

2.9 *The Way of the Spirit* John McKay, Marshall Pickering, London, England, 1988, Vol 1, p51.

2.10 *Once Saved Always Saved,* David Pawson, Hodder &

Stoughton, London, England, 1996.

2.11 Ref. 1.1, p438.

2.12 *A Theological Wordbook of the Bible*, Alan Richardson (Ed), SCM Press, London, England, 1950 p160.

2.13 Ref. 2.1, p3-124.

2.14 Ref. 2.1, p2-232.

2.15 Ref. 1.1, p390.

2.16 *The Methodist Hymn Book* The Methodist Conference, London, England, 1933, No. 362.

2.17 *Ever Increasing Faith,* Smith Wigglesworth, Gospel Publishing House, Springfield, Missouri, USA, 1971, p142.

2.18 *Unfeigned Faith* Judson Cornwall, Kingsway Publications, Eastbourne, England, 1985, p40.

Chapter 3

3.1 Ref.1.1, p435.

3.2 *Doubt: Faith in Two Minds* Os Guinness, Lion Publishing, Berkhampstead, Herts., England, 1976.

3.3 Ref: 2.5, 19 January 2001.

3.4 Ref. 2.17, p22.

Chapter 4

4.1 Ref: 2.5, 9 December 1997

4.2 Ref: 2.5, 15 January 2001.

4.3 Ref. 1.1, p193.

4.4 *Revival: Times of Refreshing* Selwyn Hughes, CWR, Farnham, Surrey, England, 1990, p23.

4.5 *Matthew Henry's Commentary on the Whole Bible*, Leslie F. Church (Ed), Marshall Morgan & Scott, Basingstoke, Hants., England, 1960, p578.

4.6 Ref. 2.16, p140.

4.7 *The Gifts of the Spirit,* Walter L. Walker (Ed), Strang Communications Co., Altamonte Springs, Florida, USA, 1992, p48.

4.8 Ref. 4.6, p50.

4.9 Ref. 2.1, p1-88.

4.10 Ref. 1.3.

4.11 *The Final Quest* Rick Joyner, Morning Star Publications, Charlotte, NC, USA, 1996, p146.

4.12 Ref.1.1, p457.

4.13 *Another Wave of Revival* Frank Bartelman, Whitaker House, Springdale, Pa, USA 1982, p79.

4.14 Quoted by Selwyn Hughes, *Every Day with Jesus* , CWR, Farnham, Surrey, England, 8 September 1997

4.15 *The Second Coming* David Pawson, Sovereign World, Tonbridge, UK, 1993, p56.

4.16 *Christianity in Crisis* Hank Hanegraaff, Word Publishing, Milton Keynes, England, 1993, p100.

4.17 Ref. 2.16, No. 977.

Chapter 5

5.1 Ref. 1.1, p150.

5.2 *The Art of Prayer* Timothy Ware (Ed), Faber & Faber, London, England, 1966, p65.

5.3 Ref. 1.3, p1. See also: *Grace & Faith* Andrew Wommack, Andrew Wommack Ministries Inc., Colorado Springs, Co, USA.

5.4 Ref. 2.16, p149.

Chapter 6

6.1 E.M. *Bounds on Prayer*, E.M. Bounds, Whitaker House, New Kensington, Pa, USA, 1997, p107.

6.2 Sermon during *Christian Praise*, Leicester, England 1996.

6.3 *Effective Fervent Prayer* Mary Alice Isleib, Mary Alice Isleib Ministries, Minneapolis, MN, USA, 1991, p172.

6.4 *The Weapons of Our Warfare,* Francis Wale Oke, Highland, Guildford, Surrey, England, 1994, p101.

6.5 Ref. 2.15, No. 223.

APPENDIX 1

A1.1 Ref. 2.16, No.372.
A1.2 Ref. 2.16, No.362.
A1.3 Ref. 2.16, No.363.
A1.4 Kingdom Faith Ministries, Horsham RH12 4RU, UK.

APPENDIX 1:
Hymns on Faith

1   *The God of love, to earth He came*
   That you might come to heaven
   Believe, believe in Jesus's name
   And all your sin's forgiven.

   Believe in Him that died for thee
   And, sure as He hath died
   The debt is paid, thy soul is free
   And thou art justified.

   Charles Wesley (1707-88)[1]

2 *Author of faith, eternal Word*
   Whose Spirit breathes the active flame
   Faith, like its Finisher and Lord
   Today as yesterday the same.

   To Thee our humble hearts aspire
   And ask the gift unspeakable
   Increase in us the kindled fire
   In us the work of faith fulfil.

   By faith we know Thee strong to save

Save us, a present Saviour Thou!
Whate'er we hope, by faith we have
Future and past subsisting now.

To him that in Thy name believes
Eternal life with Thee is given
Into himself he all receives
Pardon, and holiness, and heaven.

The things unknown to feeble sense
Unseen by reason's glimmering ray
With strong commanding evidence
Their heavenly origin display.

Faith lends its realizing light
The clouds disperse, the shadows fly
The Invisible appears in sight
And God is seen by mortal eye.

Charles Wesley (1707-88)[2]

3 *Spirit of faith, come down*
Reveal the things of God
And make to us the Godhead known
And witness with the blood.
'Tis thine the blood to apply
And give us eyes to see
Who did for every sinner die
Hath surely died for me.

No man can truly say
That Jesus is the Lord
Unless Thou take the veil away
And breathe the living word
Then, only then, we feel

Our interest in His blood
And cry with joy unspeakable
Thou art my Lord, my God!

O that the world might know
The all-atoning Lamb!
Spirit of faith, descend, and show
The virtue of His name.
The grace which all may find
The saving power impart
And testify to all mankind
And speak in every heart.

Inspire the living faith
Which whosoe'er receives
The witness in himself he hath
And consciously believes.
The faith that conquers all
And doth the mountain move
And saves whoe'er on Jesus call
And perfects them in love.

Charles Wesley (1707-88)[3]

4 *By faith we are made sons*
By faith God's chosen ones
By faith in Jesus Christ the Lord
And by faith we rest secure
By faith we are made pure
Our heavenly hope is sure by faith.

Jesus said that if we hear his word
And live out what we've heard
We can do mighty things
So we choose to trust in God above

And show our faith through love
Give him all we have.

Then in faith ask anything
In faith receive from him
In faith rely upon his word
And by faith see mountains move
By faith God's power prove
All things are possible by faith.

By faith the demons flee
By faith the blind will see
By faith the captives are set free
For by faith the weak are strong
By faith all fear is gone
All things are possible by faith.

We will live believing in his word
Declaring what we've heard
Relying on the Lord
And we'll trust in God's authority
Proclaim his majesty
Affirm Christ's victory!

Then in faith to battle go
By faith defeat the foe
By faith in Jesus Christ our King
And by faith we'll stand
By faith we'll claim this land
God's victory will prevail by faith.

(Last time)
God's kingdom will come in power by faith
All things are possible by faith.

Julian Perkins (1991)[4]

APPENDIX 2:

Questions and Exercises.

The aim of these questions and exercises is to send you to the primary source of our knowledge of the things of God - the Bible. They are not trivial questions. Their intention is to extend your study of faith beyond what you should have obtained from this little book.

A concordance is your most important study aid. Even if Bible-study software is available to you, you will often learn more by browsing through a concordance. It will sometimes suggest questions which are then more easily addressed using a computer. It is strongly recommended that you use a concordance based on the KJV. Better still, especially if you have Bible-study software on your computer, use the Greek and Hebrew dictionaries.

You should also have access to a dictionary of Bible words (e.g. ref. 2.1), and a theological word book (e.g. ref. 2.11), as well as to commentaries. An essential companion is an interlinear Greek-English NT. You may not know the Greek language, but you can learn the alphabet in an hour or two, and then look up words in a dictionary. Make sure that any Bible-study software you may have on your computer serves you and not the other way about.

Questions.
1. This book has dealt with the NT teaching on faith. What does the OT have to say about faith? Include the word 'believe' and its associates in your study. Now read Galatians 3 and tie in Paul's teaching there with your own results.

2. Write out everything Jesus said about faith, using the keywords: faith, believe and its associates; little faith, lack of faith, and unbelief. Sort these texts into groups so that you can see what he said : (a) in respect of healing; (b) about other kinds of miraculous events. What was his attitude to unbelief? How did he expect his followers to deal with unbelief?

[Hint: If you are not using a computer, it might be easiest to write each text on a small card. Then they can easily be sorted and re-sorted to reveal different things.]

3. The various NT writers had different and complementary things to say about faith. Read what the following men wrote about faith, and discover their particular emphasis. (1) James. (2) Peter. (3) The writer of Hebrews.

4. There are about 40 references to faith in Romans. Use them as a revision exercise for the subject matter of this book, apportioning each reference appropriately. Does Romans give you a balanced overview of faith?

5. Paul's letters to Timothy and Titus were written to encourage and instruct these young ministers of the gospel. What does he say to them about faith?

6. What does the OT teach about God's faithfulness?

7. Review the use of the word 'faithful' in both OT and NT. How is this word applied to (a) God, (b) man?

8. There are almost certainly areas of your Christian life for which (a) your faith is strong, but others (b) in which you struggle. Make (a) and (b) lists. Now give thanks for (a), and apply the principles of Chapter 4 to list (b).

9. Go and teach faith to someone, even your pet teddy bear. You never know a subject until you teach it.

FURTHER READING

The literature on faith is immense and very varied. The following are strongly recommended as follow-up to the present book, in no particular order.

The Holiest of All Andrew Murray, Whitaker House, Springdale, Pa, USA 1996 [First published: London, England 1895, this wonderful book is a commentary on Hebrews, of which the section dealing with Hebrews 11 is especially recommended].

Insights into Faith Andrew Wommack, Andrew Wommack Ministries Inc., Colorado Springs, Co, USA 1980. [A booklet, but one that packs an amazing amount into a small space].

Grace & Faith Andrew Wommack, Andrew Wommack Ministries Inc., Colorado Springs, Co, USA. [Totally biblical and very clear].

Faith Colin Urquhart, Sovereign World, Tonbridge, Kent, England 1992. [An excellent, clear summary study].

Faith that Overcomes the World Ulf Ekman, Word of Life Publications, Uppsala, Sweden 1992. [A sound and biblically based exposition with a practical bias].

Ever Increasing Faith Smith Wigglesworth, Gospel Publishing House, Springfield, Missouri, USA 1971. [A classic on faith by one of the great English men of faith].

Faith, What a Deal! Dave Duell, Faith Ministries Press, Greely, Co, USA 1992. [Largely anecdotal, often very funny, and definitely a worthy successor to Smith Wigglesworth].

Faith: the Link with God's Power Reinhard Bonnke, Sovereign World, Tonbridge, Kent, England 1999. [A recent treatment from one of the greatest of all evangelists].

Reckless Faith John F. MacArthur, Crossway Books, Wheaton, Ill, USA 1994. [Notable for its critique of Roman Catholic teaching. This is an extremely important book for Europeans in particular].

Those familiar with the literature on faith will appreciate that I have avoided mention of treatments originating from the so-called 'faith movement' which is largely American. It is now widely accepted that there were unfortunate emphases in that movement, such as the 'name it and claim it' style of teaching. Those who feel it necessary to go into those aspects are advised to do so with the aid of a copy of: *Christianity in Crisis* Hank Hanegraaff, Word Publishing, Milton Keynes, England, 1993.

SCRIPTURE INDEX